Christopher
COLUMBUS

Navigator to the New World

Christopher
COLUMBUS

Navigator to the New World

by
Daniel J. Carrison
Captain, USN

Franklin Watts, Inc.
575 Lexington Avenue
New York, N.Y. 10022

FIRST PRINTING

Library of Congress Catalog Card Number: 67–10333
Copyright © 1967 by Franklin Watts, Inc.
Printed in the United States of America

*This book is affectionately
dedicated to my children:
Lori; Dan; and Hank*

CONTENTS

	Page
PREFACE	ix

PART I: EARLY LIFE

1	Youth	3
2	Portugal	9
3	Isabella	19
4	Palos	27

PART II: FIRST VOYAGE

5	Historic Crossing	39
6	Island Discoveries	50
7	Triumphant Return	65

PART III: SECOND VOYAGE

8	The Fleet	75
9	Search for the Khan	85
10	Spanish Steel	95

PART IV: THIRD VOYAGE

11	Becalmed in Spain	105
12	The Gulf of Pearls	109
13	Santo Domingo	118

vii

CONTENTS

Page

PART V: FOURTH VOYAGE

14	*Spain, 1500–1502*	*129*
15	*"Gracias a Dios"*	*133*
16	*The Mosquito Coast*	*140*
17	*Beachcombers*	*149*

PART VI: DEATH

18	*"Glorious Memory"*	*161*
	Chronology	*167*
	Bibliography	*170*
	Index	*172*

PREFACE

ON St. Valentine's Day, 1493, at the height of a gale west of the Azores, a homeward-bound mariner named Christopher Columbus thought that his laboring ship would sink at any moment. Fearing that the story of his great discovery would go down with him, he wrote an account of his voyage on a piece of parchment, sealed it with waxed cloth, and tossed it overboard in an empty cask. It was never seen again.

Today that parchment would be priceless. Even though Columbus lived to tell his story in the court of Ferdinand and Isabella of Spain, much documentary evidence of his great work has been lost. Columbus was known to have been a prolific writer, but unfortunately only sixty-four pieces of his original writings are preserved today. Most of these belong to his principal living descendant and heir, the Spanish Duke of Veragua, the 17th Cristobal Colon.

Bits and pieces of Columbus' memorabilia have appeared from time to time in the 474 years that have elapsed since he first crossed the Atlantic. The appearance of each new document invariably created a stir in the historic community, and caused a new issue of literary works about the great explorer. Eighty years ago historian Henry Harrisse estimated that over 600 books and hundreds of shorter papers had been written about Columbus exclusively. It is only natural that this amount of material would represent many schools of thought and varied interpretations of his life. Columbus has been described as a pirate, a Portuguese, a Spaniard, a Greek, a Corsican, and a Catlan Jew. To some scholars he was a saint; to others he was an avaricious adventurer. Moreover, like George Washington and the tale of the cherry tree, many legends and romantic fictions about Columbus have become accepted as fact.

Those who do not credit him with the discovery of the American continent are enjoying a renewal of interest in Leif Ericson and other Viking sailors who visited our shores before Columbus. There is too much evidence to deny that certain parts of North America were visited by Europeans before 1492. But the fact remains that these visits were without significant result, and that none before Columbus established enduring contact with the New World.

This enduring contact resulting from Columbus' discovery was one of the most significant events in the history of civilization. His daring voyage into the unknown caught the imagination of the decadent Europe of that day and opened new vistas of hope about the prospects of land and opportunity in the New World. Columbus' persistence, his faith in himself, and his obstinate pursuit of a goal in the face of derisive opposition and great difficulty is an inspiring story. It was not until a generation after his death, however, that the real import of his achievement was recognized. Thereafter, according to Baron von Humboldt, "the majesty of great memories seems concentrated in the name of Christopher Columbus."

Unfortunately Columbus' life was not a "success story" in the usual meaning of the phrase. Perhaps it would have been if, after his first voyage, he had retired with the honors and riches that were heaped on him. Instead, he chose to endure the hardships of three more long voyages in a hopeless search for the elusive sea route to the Orient. In the end he died a crippled, frustrated, and discredited old man. He never knew the extent of his achievements, nor did he guess that his name would someday become the symbol of daring, of maritime competence, and of great discovery.

This book is dedicated to that symbol.

Today, as man begins the exploration of outer space, Columbus' inspired discovery is an example to cherish. There are many parallels in the two ventures, and there is the comforting thought that Columbus always returned to port safely. Saint or sinner, genius or adventurer, Columbus was, without a doubt, a courageous man and certainly one of the greatest seamen who ever lived. For those reasons alone, his story is worth retelling.

Christopher
COLUMBUS

Navigator to the New World

PART I

Early Life

CHAPTER I

YOUTH

THE truth about the birth and early life of Christopher Columbus is hard to find. There is hardly a date or a fact about his life before 1492 that has not been disputed. After he made his name illustrious, many different towns and families claimed him as their own. Most of these claims were based on nothing more than local pride and enthusiasm.

Careful research of public documents left by notaries shows that Christopher Columbus was an Italian and a native of Genoa. He was born about the year 1451, the eldest son of Domenico and Susanna Columbus, who were from respectable middle-class families. Domenico was a wool carder and weaver whose uncertain business acumen kept him on the edge of poverty during his adult life. He and his family lived alternately in Genoa and the nearby city of Savona. These two cities on the northwest coast of Italy border the Ligurian Sea which lies between Corsica and the top of Italy's boot.

At the time of Christopher's birth there were some 200 persons named Columbus living in the northwest division of Italy known as Liguria. In the capital city of Genoa, the notarial records listed four men named Domenico Columbus, but only one was a wool carder.

Moreover, the records show that there was only one Christopher Columbus living in Genoa at that time. There are sufficient statements from Christopher and his brothers, Bartholomew and Diego, to identify their father as Domenico Columbus, the weaver.

Other legal documents bear out and sustain both the parentage and birthplace of Columbus. Early historians leaned almost exclusively on a *mayorazzo*, a form of will, executed by Christopher Columbus on February 22, 1498. This legal instrument contained the following:

> "*I enjoin it upon my son, the said Don Diego, or whoever may inherit the said mayorazzo, always to keep and maintain in the City of Genoa one person of our lineage, because from thence I came and in it I was born.*"

There are several other notarial records in both Genoa and Savona which link Christopher with that area and with Domenico. For example, in 1470 Christopher co-signed a note with his father for a delivery of wine. It began, "Christofforus de Columbo, son of Domenico, over 19 years old, in the presence, and by the authority, advice and consent of the said Domenico, his father present and approving. . . ." Here he acknowledged the debt for wine in the presence of witnesses, and he and his father swore to abide by the terms of the note.

At other times Christopher appeared before a notary to witness a will (1472), to purchase wool jointly with his father (1472), and to attest to a bill of sale for the family house (1473).

Why, then, should there be any doubt about the explorer's origin? Actually, Christopher Columbus himself is somewhat at fault for this doubt, and so is his youngest son Ferdinand. During his later years, Christopher made several misleading statements about his early life. Ferdinand Columbus, who wrote one of the first biographies of Christopher Columbus, admitted some confusion in tracing his father as a youth and young man. He wrote his book twenty-five years after Christopher had died, when he himself was a wealthy man of position. It is suspected that he preferred to let his father's humble beginning remain obscure.

Insofar as Columbus, the rest of his immediate family, and his contemporaries were concerned, there was no doubt about his origin. It was much later, when some scholars seized upon some uncertainties of Ferdinand and Oviedo, another early biographer, that doubts appeared. Their contrary statements have been disparaged with time, and the lingering doubts rather well dispelled. Historian Samuel Eliot Morison, the best-known current authority on Columbus, dismisses these other claims as inconsequential and states unequivocally that now, "there is no mystery about the birth, family or race of Christopher Columbus." The record bears him out.

This record, which has been painstakingly gathered through several centuries, is almost a blank during a great part of Columbus' youth. When the thread of his history appears intact again, he is mature, speaks Portuguese and Spanish, and has developed skill as a seaman and a mapmaker. From his own statements we know that he went to sea at the age of fourteen. This was not an unusually early age for such a venture— boys even younger than that had been going to sea since time began.

It must have been an exciting adventure for young Christopher. Fifteenth century merchant trade in the Mediterranean was a rough calling. Ships from different nations or city-states preyed on one another. A sailor was expected to be as handy with a sword as he was with a marlin spike. Notwithstanding the practices of piracy and high-handedness on the sea, Columbus must have accepted a sailor's life as a happy alternative to his father's wool business. He became a proficient seaman and earned the equivalent of master's papers while he was still in his twenties. He voyaged from one end of the Mediterranean to the other and even ventured past the Straits of Gibraltar for an occasional blue-water cruise in the Atlantic. By the time Christopher was thirty, he had become a master seaman and a qualified ship commander. Somewhere along the way he was introduced to map making—a profession which, at the very least, required a knowledge of geography and mathematics as well as dexterity with drawing instruments and good penmanship.

The Genoese had great reputations as mariners. Their ships plied the farthest seas, and Genoese fleets were sought by kings and princes of Europe for aid in their perpetual wars against each other. Columbus grew up and flourished in his new calling, at a time when "the bold youth of Genoa were covered with wounds and glory on so many seas."

In later life, Columbus told an interesting story of an expedient he used to take an unwilling crew into battle. As the story goes, Columbus was the master of a ship that sailed for the French in the war of René of Anjou against Alphonso V of Aragon. "King René," Columbus said, "sent me to Tunis to capture the galley *Fernandina*, and when I arrived off the island of St. Pedro, in Sardinia, I was informed that there were two ships and a carrack with the galley; by which intelligence my crew were so troubled that they determined to proceed no further, but to return to Marseilles for another vessel and more people; as I could not by any means compel them, I assented apparently to their wishes, altering the point of the compass and spreading all sail. It was then evening, and the next morning we were within the Cape of Carthagena, while all were firmly of the opinion that they were sailing toward Marseilles."

Just what his crew said and did that morning at Tunis is not recorded. They may have fought bravely, shouting their Genoese battle cry, "Viva San Georgio!" or they may have prevailed upon their captain to retreat and seek reinforcements at Marseilles. Their conduct is not important, but the fact that Columbus could deceive his crew is signally interesting. It is the first example of his stubborn will as well as his versatility at sea. As we shall see, he practiced a similar trick on the crew of the *Santa Maria* in 1492, or else he would never have sighted land on October 12.

Columbus did not spend all of his early years entirely at sea. Somewhere he found time to pick up a fair education. Ferdinand asserts that his father attended the University of Pavia, but there is no record of this. From time to time, between voyages, he must have returned home, for how else could his name appear on various notarial records between the years 1470 and 1473?

His younger brother Bartholomew settled in Lisbon, the chief center of navigational science in Europe, where he earned a living making maps and globes.

Columbus joined him there about 1476 in a manner that has been much debated. The more glamorous story has it that the merchant ship in which he traveled was sunk in a fight with the French off Cape St. Vincent, and that he abandoned ship, found an oar for buoyancy, and swam two leagues to the Portuguese shore near Lagos. This account is accepted by many responsible historians, but others point out that the story cannot be documented. These authors prefer to believe that Columbus made his way to Lisbon in some legitimate and unspectacular merchant assignment, and then decided to cast his lot with his brother Bartholomew. No matter which version we choose, Columbus' journey to Lisbon was important, for it was there that he first conceived his idea of a westward passage to the Orient.

CHAPTER 2

PORTUGAL

WHEN Columbus arrived in Lisbon, Portugal was at the height of her golden age of exploration. The influence of Prince Henry the Navigator had drawn many of the world's foremost mariners to Portugal early in the fifteenth century. Spurred by Henry's zeal to find the southern cape of Africa (and thus a sea route to India) seamen and astronomers gathered at his observatory at Sagres to promote the science of navigation and to plan ever-lengthening voyages down the African coast. In 1434, one of Prince Henry's captains finally pushed past Cape Bojador. In succeeding years, others explored farther down the coast, discovering the Canary Islands and probing as far as the Gold Coast. When Prince Henry died in 1460 without realizing his ambition, his enthusiasm for discovery was transferred to some of the many explorers whom he had sponsored and supported, who were more than willing to carry on his great work.

The fame of the Portuguese explorations spread through Europe. Commercial enterprises followed quickly on the heels of each fresh discovery, and the docks at Lisbon groaned under the weight of exciting new produce. The city's inhabitants never ceased to marvel at the number of ships that would gather in the Tagus River, or at the frequency with which they would catch the swift flood tide, drop past Estoril, cross the bar, and head out into the blue Atlantic. Money-lenders, scholars, and adventurers joined with grizzled seamen to make Lisbon the new center of nautical and commercial progress and, if not the richest city in Europe, the most exciting.

Lisbon was a Mecca for Christopher Columbus who by now was a fully matured and seasoned merchant sailor. In this exciting and inspiring atmosphere he was driven to new studies. He learned Portuguese and Spanish, studied Latin, and spent many hours pouring over the latest books on navigation. He also slowly accumulated an estate.

In his twenties, Columbus has been described as a striking-looking man of "noble and commanding presence." He had a fair, ruddy complexion and was powerfully built. His friends thought that he was both courteous and cordial, well-read, and an excellent conversationalist. There is little doubt that he was an impressive figure, for throughout his life he was able to obtain audiences with the most influential persons in the societies and governments of Portugal and Spain.

It did not take him long to find a wife. At a chapel in Lisbon he met the charming Felipa Moniz de Perestrello, daughter of sea captain Bartholomew Perestrello, who had sailed under Prince Henry and had been rewarded for his efforts with the hereditary governorship of the island of Porto Santo, which lies in the Madeira Islands. Señor Perestrello had died some years before, so Felipa and her mother resided alone in the family house at Lisbon. In marrying Felipa, Columbus did well. The Perestrellos were a distinguished family with an enviable and secure social position. They were not wealthy, but they did have the governorship of Porto Santo and an island estate to fall back on.

They were married in 1479 in Lisbon, but soon moved to Porto Santo and the peace and quiet of the country. Widow Perestrello catered to her new son-in-law's interest in the sea and navigation by giving him her late husband's charts, journals, navigation books, and instruments. Las Casas, one of the earliest and best biographers of Columbus, believed that the explorer learned a great deal from Perestrello's papers. He studied the Portuguese method of navigation carefully, and was so impressed, says Las Casas, that "he sailed with Portguese crews as if he had been one of them."

While Felipa and Christopher lived in Porto Santo they had a child, whom they called Diego. Columbus was delighted to have a male heir, and throughout his life he was careful to see that the proceeds of his voyages were guarded for his descendants. As a matter of fact, he was so occupied with the male side of his family that he later willed everything to "Diego and his male heirs"; otherwise his estate was to pass to his illegitimate son Ferdinand, who was born in Spain several years after Felipa had died.

Their sojourn in Madeira was a happy and profitable one. From time to time Columbus followed his rover instinct and would sail away on an attractive voyage. The number of his trips is not known, but his contemporaries recalled that he mentioned experiences gained while sailing down the west coast of Africa to Guinea. Whenever he was home for any length of time, he continued his studies and maintained contact with the sea by visiting ships that called at Funchal with news of new discoveries.

His son Ferdinand insists that it was at Porto Santo that Columbus formed his basic ideas of a westward passage to the Orient. He was intrigued whenever the west wind piled up great surf on the island's beaches. He would look for hours at the strange bits of flotsam and jetsam that were borne in with the tide. There were pieces of bamboo, strange wooden debris, carvings, and "sea beans," the like of which could not be found anywhere in Europe. Here he had unmistakable evidence that there was land somewhere to the west. Even today these things are periodically cast up on the shores of Porto Santo and on the beaches of Ireland as well.

This visible evidence, which was borne to Columbus' door by the Gulf Stream, served to corroborate what he had learned through study. It was no secret that he was intrigued with the idea of a westward passage to the Indies; and, as a matter of fact, this concept had been an intellectual toy of scholars for nearly seventeen centuries. Among the learned men who had believed this venture to be feasible were Aristotle, Ptolemy, and Roger Bacon, the English philosopher. First Aristotle concluded that the world was a sphere, and not a very big one at that. He noticed that the altitude of the North Star (Polaris) was different when measured from various places of observation on the earth's surface. He therefore concluded that the earth could not be flat, and then theorized that India could be reached by traveling west of Gibraltar over a single sea.

Two hundred years before Columbus moved to Porto Santo, Roger Bacon collected ancient papers to prove that the distance from Europe to the Orient was not as great as others thought. These papers were assembled and published in book form by Petrus Alliarcus in 1410 under the title *Imago Mundi*. This book was immensely popular during the age of discovery, and it soon became one of Columbus' favorites. The explorer's own copy, liberally annotated with his own handwriting, is still preserved in the Biblioteca Colombina in Seville.

Among the ancient predictions and prophecies that entranced Columbus were learned treatises and calculations of the earth's size. He studied these carefully and then selected the one which suited his purposes best. The first recorded estimate in the history of man was made by a Greek astronomer, Eratosthenes (276–196 B.C.), who came up with the surprisingly accurate figure of 59.5 miles per degree of longitude at the equator. Since the entire globe covers only 360 degrees, the earth's circumference can be found by multiplying 360 by the number of miles in a degree. The figure obtained by using the correct distance of 60 miles per degree is 21,600 nautical miles (roughly 25,000 English statute miles).

In the second century A.D., Ptolemy and others made similar calculations and added their own estimates of the amount of land that rested on the earth's surface. After the journeys of Marco Polo, this figure was overestimated, and China was credited with about one fourth more landmass than it truly entails. These early calculations also made a gross error in the location of Japan, which was then known as Cipangu. These guesses placed Nippon about one thousand miles to the east of its true position. Columbus eagerly seized upon each error that seemed to shorten the length of the western passage. He finally ended up with a figure of 45 miles per degree, underestimating the total distance by about 25 per cent. His mistake would certainly have caused the death of all in his first voyage if the New World had not lain between the coasts of Europe and China. Thirty years later, Magellan almost destroyed his crew in exploring the Pacific and sailing across the great distance that separated the New World and China. He sailed for weeks across the Pacific and his men nearly died of thirst and starvation, yet his ships were much better equipped than were the *Niña*, the *Pinta*, and the *Santa Maria*.

Right or wrong, Columbus believed in his great idea, and it soon became an obsession with him. At about this time he corresponded with one of the famous astronomers of his day, Toscanelli of Florence. This exchange of letters between a widely known astronomer and a relatively unknown mariner was important. It gave Columbus stature and lent credence to his arguments.

This famous exchange came about in this manner: At the urging of King Alfonso V of Portugal, a clergyman of Lisbon named Fernam Martins had corresponded with Paolo (Paul) Toscanelli on the subjects of Portuguese commerce with Africa and navigation on the high seas. Columbus heard of this and asked an Italian friend to carry a letter from him to Toscanelli. He received a reply written in Latin, which contained a copy of an earlier letter that Toscanelli had written to Martins as well as a copy of a map which he had prepared from the descriptions of Marco Polo's travels:

"*Paul, the physicist, to Christopher Columbus greeting. I perceive your great and noble desire to go to the place where the spices grow: wherefore in reply to a letter of yours, I send you a copy of another letter, which I wrote a few days ago (or some time ago) to a friend of mine, a gentleman of the household of the most gracious king of Portugal before the wars of Castile, in reply to another, which by command of His Highness he wrote me concerning that matter: and I send you another sailing chart, similar to the one I sent him, by which your demands will be satisfied. The copy of that letter of mine is as follows . . .*"

Toscanelli's chart showed the coasts of Asia to be much closer to Europe than earlier charts had shown, and he placed Japan and a mysterious island named "Antilla" even closer. The letter to Martins said,

"*I have formerly spoken with you about a shorter route to the places of the spices by ocean navigation than you are pursuing by Guinea . . . I have decided to exhibit that route by means of a sailing chart . . . upon which are laid down your coasts, and the islands from which you must begin to shape your course steadily westward, and the places at which you are bound to arrive, and how far from the pole or the equator you ought to keep away . . . through how many miles you are to travel . . .*"

Toscanelli wrote his letter to Martins in 1474, and sent a copy to Columbus in 1481 or 1482. The impact on Columbus was immediate. Here was the final answer to his problem—the key that solved the puzzle. In all of his subsequent petitions for support of his western passage he leaned heavily on Toscanelli's chart. As we shall see, in 1492, when he finally set out on his historic first voyage, he carried out the physicist's sailing instructions to the letter.

At about the time when this exchange of letters took place, Columbus completed an important voyage to the north. To many scholars this is one of the most controversial events of his life. In a letter which is quoted by his son Ferdinand and Las Casas he described it as follows:

> *"In the month of February 1477, I sailed a hundred leagues beyond the island of Thule [Iceland] an island of which the south part is in latitude 73° not 63°, as some say; and it does not lie within Ptolemy's western boundary, but much farther west. And to this island, which is as big as England, the English go with their wares, especially from Bristol. When I was there the sea was not frozen. In some places the tide rose and fell twenty-six fathoms."*

Remembering that many quotations of Columbus have been translated from Spanish to Latin to Italian to English, it can be assumed that something was changed in the process. For example, twenty-six fathoms is one hundred fifty-six feet; there is no place in the world with a tidal range of that magnitude. Iceland lies between latitudes 64° and 67° north, but mariners in Columbus' day often made tremendous errors in celestial navigation. Rather than try to pick the quotation to pieces, or to interpret it as having mysterious meanings, it is best to accept it as reasonable evidence that Columbus made a voyage into the extremes of the North Atlantic. This rounded out his apprenticeship and gave him the right to speak with experience.

As boy and man he had sailed over all of the known oceans. He had covered the Mediterranean from one end to the other. He had sailed the Atlantic from the Gold Coast of Africa to the frozen shores of Iceland. He had been as far west as Madeira and the Azores. As a result of this experience, Columbus could mingle on equal terms with any gathering of seamen from the wharves of Genoa to the docks of Lisbon. And in addition, he was a mapmaker and scholar, having spent almost as many hours in study as he had on the quarterdeck. Columbus was ready—but no one would listen.

The period from 1484 to 1485 was a tragic one for Columbus. First King John of Portugal secretly deceived him, and then his wife, Felipa, died. Little is known about Felipa's death, but the combination of her passing and the shabby treatment he received in the court of King John persuaded Columbus to leave Portugal.

Columbus' plan for a western passage was submitted to the Portuguese king in 1484. At first the king's advisers summarily rejected it, but John referred the proposal to another conference of learned men in order to be sure. These mathematicians and astronomers soon saw the errors of Columbus' calculations, but some were so impressed with the mariner's arguments that they believed that the voyage was feasible. John, therefore, received the divided opinion that the idea of a voyage west was impractical, but it might be worth trying. Accordingly, he secretly sent out a ship with instructions to try out the sailing plans of Columbus. The captain of that vessel did not have the convictions of Columbus. A few days' westward sailing in high latitudes with unfavorable winds were enough for him, and he returned to Lisbon posthaste, ridiculing the whole idea.

When Columbus learned of this unworthy effort, he dropped all attempts to sail for Portugal and left for Spain in righteous anger. He was convinced that he was right: the earth was round, and the shortest route to the Indies was westward, across the Atlantic. If the Portuguese would not believe him, perhaps the Spaniards would.

CHAPTER 3

ISABELLA

THE exact date is uncertain, but sometime in the year 1485, Columbus and his young son Diego boarded a ship in Lisbon and took passage south to the small port of Palos, Spain. Their arrival was unnoticed, for no one had the power of prophecy or foresight to connect this event with the epochal discovery of the New World.

Spain was on the threshhold of greatness. The fortunate union of Ferdinand and Isabella in 1469 had merged the kingdoms of Aragon and Castile. Sixteen years later, when Columbus arrived in Spain, these two capable rulers had stamped out the internal wars that had weakened and divided the country for years. Now a united Spain supported the crown, whose immediate and most important task was to drive the Moors from Granada, the mountain stronghold of the Mohammedans. Thanks to Columbus, Spain was about to inherit the wealth of the New World, which would enable her to rise above internal problems to become mistress of Europe and pioneer conqueror of the Americas.

Some of the more romantic versions of Columbus' life make a great deal of Isabella's support for his voyage.

The story about her offer to sell her crown jewels to finance his expedition has no basis of fact. She was much too shrewd to have to resort to that expedient. Actually, she was very clever in spreading the cost of the expedition, and even persuaded Columbus to put up some money himself.

Isabella's relation to the voyages of discovery stemmed from her unusual position as a co-ruler of Spain. When she married Ferdinand she retained her hereditary right to rule the kingdom of Castile and kept her own council and officials. On the other hand, Ferdinand remained the ruler of Aragon. Yet the two jointly ruled Spain, issuing decrees that bore both signatures. This picturesque couple gave Spain the leadership and inspiration that launched her on the path to glory.

Ferdinand of Aragon was an ambitious ruler who had an unusual flair for diplomacy. He was obsessed with affairs of state and is credited with being one of the most subtle and skillful monarchs who ever sat on a throne. At the same time he was a bigoted religious fanatic. It was he who installed the dreaded Inquisition in Spain and expelled the Jews.

His wife, consort, and co-ruler was one of the most attractive noblewomen of history. Beautiful, pious Isabella had a natural grace and dignity. She loved Spain and continually strove for reforms that would bind disparate factions together and ensure a united country. She took an active part in governmental affairs, sitting on councils with ability and authority equal to her husband's. While he concentrated on state and military matters, she leaned toward the improvement of knowledge, sponsoring those skilled in letters and arts. Thus it was she, and not Ferdinand, who was more interested in and sympathetic toward Columbus.

It took almost a year before Columbus had his first audience with the royal couple. But in the meantime he had won over many influential supporters. When he first landed at Palos, chance led him to the monastery of La Ribida, where he appeared on foot one hot dusty day with little Diego in tow. The story goes that he knocked at the gate and asked the porter for some bread and water for the boy. Here he met Brother Antonio de Marchena, an astronomer of note, who quickly took a friendly interest in Columbus and his bold plan. He advised the tattered mariner to try his luck with certain of the powerful dukes nearby, and gave him a letter of introduction.

Columbus then set out on a frustrating campaign that was to last seven years. It was a bitter period in his life, but he steadfastly argued his case, suffering ridicule and enduring many false hopes and disappointments. His first contact in Cordova was with Don Enrique de Guzman, who passed the interesting mariner on to Luis de la Cerda, the Duke of Medina Celi. The duke offered to support Columbus' voyage forthwith, but soon had second thoughts, and suggested that the king's approval would be required for such a meaningful discovery effort. Accordingly, Medina Celi wrote Isabella that he had extended the hospitality of his house to a Genoese sailor named Cristóbal Colón (the Spanish adaptation of Christopher Columbus), and that this man was convinced that he could find a new, short ocean route to India. Medina Celi added that he was willing to fit out the expedition at his own expense, but hesitated to do so without the crown's approval. The reply from Isabella was long coming, but she asked the duke to send Columbus to her.

In January, 1486, Columbus arrived in Cordova,

but it was not until May that he had his first royal audience. Ferdinand and Isabella were favorably impressed, but not won over completely. They decided to submit Columbus' plan to their counselors, and placed him, in the meanwhile, on a modest royal stipend. Actually, Columbus was fortunate to get this much attention. The war against the Moors was first on everyone's mind; Ferdinand and Isabella were in the midst of preparations for the coming summer campaign.

Fernando de Talavera, who was a powerful man of the church and Queen Isabella's confessor, served as president of the board that reviewed the plan. These learned men did not need to be convinced that the earth was round. Throughout the hearings there was one unassailable fact that could not be dispelled by emotion, quotations, or the magnetic personality of Columbus. He had calculated the distance wrong. The skilled mathematicians discovered this and concluded that the plan was impracticable. No crew could survive a journey of 10,000 miles—the approximate distance from the Canary Islands to China. Yet this council ended up with the same conclusion as the Junta dos Mathematicos of Lisbon. They were so impressed with the zeal and ardor of this Italian sailor that they rendered an inconclusive report to Ferdinand and Isabella.

All of this took time. There were many meetings, and there was a war to be won. Columbus was retained in their majesties' service, but he remained an unhappy foreigner who lingered on the fringes of the court.

It was during this time that he "formed a connection" with a lady of Cordova, Beatriz Enríquez de Arana. In August, 1488, she bore him a son, whom they named Ferdinand. Columbus always recognized the responsibility of this union, but he never married Beatriz. In his will he directed his legitimate son Diego to look after her, charging him to see that she had "a way to live honorably." Their son Ferdinand lived to become a man of wealth, the owner of a library of 10,000 volumes, and one of the most quoted biographers of his famous father.

Shortly after Ferdinand was born, Columbus returned to Lisbon. There he met his brother Bartholomew, who had just returned from the exciting voyage to the Cape of Good Hope with the Portuguese discoverer, Bartholomew Dias. The two brothers hit upon a plan that would give them a better chance of success. Columbus was to remain in Spain and continue to plead his cause while Bartholomew journeyed to England and France to see if support could be found there. Neither King Henry VII of England nor King Charles VIII of France would give a definite Yes. Negotiations slowed to a standstill. In Spain, Ferdinand and Isabella informed Columbus that they would reconsider his project after the war in Granada was over.

By now Columbus' hair had turned snowy white. He had forsaken position, profession, and family to overcome opposition to his great enterprise. In 1491, half persuaded now to leave Spain to try his luck in France, he visited Diego at the monastery of La Ribida. During this visit he met the prior, Juan Perez, who listened attentively to his story. The monk begged Columbus not to leave Spain. As a former father-confessor to Isabella, he was not without influence. He introduced Columbus to Martín Alonzo Pinzón, an experienced sailor and shipowner of Palos. Among these new acquaintances Columbus found support and encouragement. He agreed to stay at La Ribida while Perez negotiated with Isabella for another hearing.

At last there seemed to be hope. Isabella invited Juan Perez to come to her camp near Granada. When he returned to Palos he brought with him an invitation for Columbus to visit Isabella, and 20,000 maravedis * to subsidize the journey. Christopher purchased a new suit of clothes and a mule and set out for the royal camp. There he found a cordial welcome and willing listeners, but once again he was put off "until the war is over." He did not have long to wait. Spain's great victory at Granada came on January 2, 1492. King Ferdinand became completely engrossed with military and diplomatic affairs, so Isabella took up negotiations with Columbus.

To Isabella, this strange man was hard to understand. For years he had pled his case, lived on charity, and forsaken every comfort, and here he was, as proud as ever, even to the point of demanding that he be made an admiral and hereditary viceroy of any lands that he might discover. What was worse, he wanted a share of all revenues that might come from these lands. He was impossible. Talavera advised the queen to refuse, and she did.

Once more a sad Columbus prepared to depart. This time he fully intended to leave Spain forever. On the day that he mounted his mule and headed for Cordova, an inexplicable thing happened. Isabella exercised her woman's prerogative and changed her mind! It is said that Luis de Santangel, one of the few remaining supporters of Columbus in the Spanish court, obtained an

*Spanish copper coins of that period, worth about one-third of a cent each.

audience with the queen and persuaded her that great glory would come from a voyage to spread Christianity to the heathens. Columbus' enterprise, therefore, had taken on a religious aspect which now was more important than gold and spices or new territorial acquisitions. Isabella sent a swift messenger to summon Columbus back to court.

The next three months were the most satisfactory ones that Columbus had ever spent in the Spanish court. The legal preparations were time-consuming but thorough. Columbus was promised the titles of Admiral of the Oceans and Viceroy and Governor-General over all islands and continents that he discovered. These hereditary titles were to pass to his heirs perpetually. Moreover, it was agreed that he would be entitled to one-tenth of "all pearls, precious stones, gold, silver, spices and merchandise" that issued from his admiralty. And lastly, he could "contribute an eighth part of the expense in fitting out vessels to sail on this enterprise, and receive an eighth part of the profits."

Financing the expedition was a difficult matter, and it is true that Isabella at first thought of pledging her crown jewels. This was not required, however. Luis de Santangel contributed a healthy loan; then a canny court official remembered that the town of Palos had been suspected of smuggling—or some other misdemeanor. Accordingly that port city was assessed the cost of two vessels for the expedition. Some friends of Columbus loaned him the money for one eighth of the cost; the remainder came from the royal treasury.

Thus, after years of waiting, Columbus had overcome the first great obstacle. His enterprise had been approved and financed, and he had in his possession a signed contract in which the crown charged him to "discover and acquire certain islands and mainland in the ocean sea."

So Columbus left Granada for Palos with a light heart and, no doubt, a deep gratitude for woman's intuition.

CHAPTER 4

PALOS

CONCURRENT with obtaining approval of his voyage, Columbus also became a public figure. No longer did he move in the obscurity that has plagued his biographers for almost 500 years. From the year 1492 there is ample evidence to describe his voyages, his thoughts, his strengths, and his weaknesses. While Columbus was a confident, superb seaman who earned the admiration of all who sailed with him, the great explorer was at the same time a poor administrator. As an admiral and seaman Columbus ranks with the greatest, but as a governor-general he was inept. In his own time his superiors became so obsessed with his faults and the administrative problems he created that they soon forgot the magnificence of his discoveries and the great courage that had made them possible.

Actually, Columbus had achieved a fantastic triumph before he even got his feet wet. By sheer obstinacy and a tenacious belief in his enterprise he had won a great victory in Granada. On the basis of his personality alone, he and a handful of supporters had overcome the objections of the wisest men in the Kingdom of Spain and persuaded two bankrupt rulers to finance a voyage of doubtful value. On top of this, he, a foreigner, demanded and had been promised the hereditary title of admiral and the right to call himself "Don." Moreover, these titles, as well as a share of the wealth that might come from his discoveries, were accorded to him and his family in perpetuity.

The degree to which Ferdinand and Isabella had fallen under his spell is evident in the official proclamations that got the voyage under way in the sleepy port of Palos. The first was a royal order to the townspeople. On May 23, 1492, Columbus and Friar Juan Perez met some town authorities and many of its residents at the church of St. George in Palos. There a notary read the royal command which obliged the town of Palos to prepare two caravels (small sailing vessels) for sea within ten days, and to put the ships and crews under Columbus' command, to sail with him as he directed. The order stated that the crews should be paid four months' wages in advance, at the usual rates for seamen serving in armed vessels. It further provided that upon receipt of a certificate signed by Columbus attesting his satisfaction, the town of Palos would be considered to have discharged its obligation to the crown.

Another decree ordered suspension of criminal proceedings against any man who signed on with Columbus —the suspension to last for the duration of the voyage and for two months after the return. Two more decrees dealt with the problem of supplies. Palos and neighboring towns were enjoined to provide supplies and services to Columbus at reasonable prices without delay. Local officials were cautioned that these supplies should be transported and delivered tax free.

Each of these decrees and orders carried a "penalty

clause" which levied a fine of 10,000 maravedis upon anyone committing an infraction of them. For the crown had anticipated trouble and had thus provided against any local embargo or strike in the preparations for the voyage. But no one really anticipated the great dismay and reluctance that swept the area when the ships' destination was announced. Decree or no decree, seamen hid in the hills and refused to sign on. In Palos and the adjoining town of Moguer recruiting efforts brought jeers, complaints, and near-riot. No one wanted to sail into the "sea of darkness" where there were untold dangers and sea monsters that defied description. Weeks dragged by with little general improvement. Finally, on June 20, the king issued a decree to seize and impress vessels and crews. He sent Juan de Penalosa, an energetic officer of his royal court, to see that this order was carried out.

These drastic measures might have prevailed in the end, but the path was cleared and preparations accelerated when Martín Alonzo Pinzón, a successful sea captain of Palos, volunteered to sail with Columbus. This was a providential turn of events; the Pinzóns were respected mariners, well known along the entire Spanish coast. Martín, joined by his brother Vicente, cooperated and exerted great influence. Within a month everything was ready.

To readers of the twentieth century, it is difficult to imagine the actual conditions of life at sea in the fifteenth century—what the ships were like and how the crews sailed them. By today's standards one can only marvel that Columbus even sailed over the horizon, let alone completed a voyage of 3,300 miles into an unknown sea.

The town of Palos provided two caravels, the *Niña*

and the *Pinta*. The *Santa Maria*, a somewhat larger vessel, similar to a Mediterranean carrack, was chartered by Columbus from its owner, Juan de la Cosa. Columbus chose the 110-ton *Santa Maria* as his flagship. She was more comfortable but she had a greater draft and proved to be a clumsy, lumbering sailer. Her dimensions were a mere 80 feet in length and 25 feet in width, yet she was much larger than the *Niña* and *Pinta*.

Early in 1966, a replica of the *Santa Maria* arrived in Washington, D. C., and moored at the foot of Main Avenue. During bright sunlight this latter-day *Santa Maria* is a gay, attractive sight with picturesque banners streaming in the wind. But on rainy winter nights she looks forlorn, uncomfortable, and ungainly. To stand on the deck of the *Santa Maria* under those desolate conditions, with water lapping against her sides, and feel the slight motion of the ship from the wavelets of the Potomac Basin, is about as close as one can get today to the circumstances of Columbus' time.

This model was built in Barcelona, Spain, under the direction of Jose Maria Martinez-Hidalgo y Teran, the curator of the Barcelona Maritime Museum. After nine years of research, Teran completed plans of the *Santa Maria* which are probably more accurate than any that have been made before. The ship was built by craftsmen who had learned the shipbuilding skills of the fifteenth century; they used the tools, patterns, and forms of that time. Flags and sails were woven on the looms of that day, and all rope and cordage was made on a "rope walk" which was constructed for that purpose. The fittings and furniture, from wine kegs to tables, from the sandbox "cookstove" to Columbus' bunk, are all authentic handmade copies of museum pieces.

Judging from this model as well as others, the *Santa Maria* looked swaybacked and stubby, with her high stern and high forecastle separated by a short waist. She had three masts; the tallest (the mainmast) was 80 feet from its foundation in the ship's keel to its peak above the crow's nest. The *Santa Maria* rolled and pitched at sea, she steered badly, and she frequently took water over the bow. Her hold was filled with stores, so that there were no living spaces for the crew. In the custom of the day, sailors would bed down on deck, huddled in their cloaks against some part of the ship that would break the wind and shield them from spray. It was different in the sterncastle, where Columbus lived. The Admiral had a built-in bunk suitably draped for privacy, and in the center of his cabin he had a desk and chair. This is where he spread his charts and worked on his journals.

Ships of the fifteenth century sailed best with the wind on the quarter. Because of their rigs and rounded bottoms they had difficulty sailing close to the wind, and could make very little headway against a combination of wind and current. For most voyages they had to steer zigzag courses to make headway in a given direction. During his first voyage, Columbus sailed south from Palos to pick up the trade winds which were favorable for almost the entire outward leg. As a matter of fact, the winds were so favorable for a westerly heading that his sailors were afraid that they would never be able to return to Spain against the steady North East Trades.

The smaller *Niña* and *Pinta* were ships of about 55 to 60 tons. *Niña* was originally equipped with lateen (triangular-shaped) sails, but she was rerigged with square sails for the ocean crossing. After the *Santa Maria* grounded off Haiti, Columbus chose *Niña* for the return voyage. *Pinta*, fastest of the three ships, was used for exploitation by Martín Alonzo Pinzón, who sailed off by himself to look for gold when Columbus left Cuba. During the outward leg he kept pressing on ahead in hopes of making the first landfall and thereby claiming the reward offered by the crown.

A total of 90 men were needed to man the three ships; *Santa Maria* had 40, *Pinta* 26, and *Niña* 24. Contrary to some accounts, only four of these were convicts who took advantage of the royal decree which allowed immunity for the voyage. Martín Alonzo Pinzón commanded the *Pinta*, while his younger brother, Vicente, commanded the *Niña*. Both of these men were experienced seamen whose reputations attracted other good men to sign on. Without their help, Columbus might never have recruited a crew. (However, had he known that the Pinzón family would enter into court proceedings against him after his death, he might have demurred. This unsuccessful attempt to strip Columbus' heirs of hereditary titles and income is not one of the brightest pages of Spanish history.)

In the fifteenth century, the rising interest in voyages of discovery down the coast of Africa, west to the Azores, and north to Iceland, had created a competent body of seamen along the Atlantic seaboard. Before 1492, when Portugal was in the ascendancy, many of the world's ablest seamen gathered in Lisbon. It was only natural that some of these men migrated to the Spanish, French, English, and Dutch fleets, spreading their knowledge of blue-water sailing. Thus, when Columbus recruited crews for his small fleet, he obtained experienced sailors who were not frightened when land disappeared over the horizon. Except for the poor seamanship that caused the loss of the *Santa Maria,* these men gave a good account of themselves, particularly during the storms encountered on the return voyage.

Some historians credit the invention of the astrolabe as the main reason for Columbus' successful navigation. However, Rear Admiral Samuel E. Morison, a seaman as well as a historian, has shown such great errors in the discoverer's "celestial" navigation that this claim has little value. It is true that the cross staff and astrolabe did permit crude measurements of the altitude of a heavenly body (and thereby a rough estimate of latitude), but the great pilots of the fifteenth century were dead-reckoning sailors, not celestial navigators. Celestial navigation was practiced by learned mathematicians and astronomers, not all of whom could handle a sailing ship, let alone command a rough and ready crew. In this connection it is interesting to note that 270 years after the first voyage of Columbus, the celebrated English discoverer Captain James Cook took an astronomer along with him on two of his great voyages.

Columbus was a master at dead-reckoning navigation. No one can take that away from him, and today's navigators, who depend on modern instruments, accurate timepieces, depth finders, and radar, can only wonder at his skill. Columbus used the mariner's magnetic compass for direction and actually estimated his speed through the water, by, as it were, "the seat of his pants." With this crude beginning he would lay down his track for the length of time that the sandglass indicated, and plot the course and distance made good. Of course, he added refinements for "set" and "drift"—the distance that his round-bottomed ship would slide off course due to the force of the wind and ocean current. This sort of refinement, or "sixth sense," of the navigator, was what separated great pilots from the ordinary ones. They applied it when they had evidence of it, but realized that at times drift was impossible to measure. Yet it was with such crude methods that Columbus made repeated trips to the Indies and returned home in remarkable time. On his first return he stopped at the Azores for water, no small feat in view of the bad weather that accompanied him on this leg. On other voyages he raised the coast of Spain or Portugal within a respectable distance of his intended landfall.

Having been a mapmaker by trade, Columbus had collected for his trip one of the finest set of navigational charts available. From his earlier correspondence with Toscanelli, he had this famed astronomer's map with him. It was on the strength of this, as well as his own conviction, that he planned a westerly course from the Canaries for Cipangu (Japan).

By early August, 1492, Columbus was almost ready. Having placed his son in the court at Madrid, where he served as page to Prince Juan, the heir apparent, Columbus turned his full energy toward his ships, his men, and his religion. In addition to the two Pinzón captains he shipped several other notable men of the area. First there was another Pinzón, Francisco Martín, who served as pilot of the *Pinta*. There were three other pilots, Bartolomeo Rolan, Sancho Ruiz, and Pedro Alonzo Niño. Each ship had a surgeon, and there were other minor officials to carry out important "landsmen" duties. There was a notary to make an official record of important events and a historian to prepare a concurrent narrative. Luis de Torres, a skilled linguist, was aboard to assist Columbus in discussions with the Great Khan, whom he hoped to find in Cathay. In addition, there were two officials from the royal court who supervised expenditures. Notably, there were no priests on the first voyage.

The ships were loaded with enough provisions, wine, and water to last about 40 days. Columbus topped off liquids and ordered some fresh meat in the Canaries. Otherwise the standard diet consisted of the following staples: salt meat, cheese, salt fish, olive oil, hardtack bread, sea biscuits, beans, sugar, rice, honey, and raisins.

During the centuries that have elapsed since the Admiral's first voyage, time has dimmed one of the glowing purposes of his enterprise: to carry Christianity to the heathens. Apparently Columbus believed that this mission was equally as important as finding the gold and spices of the Indies. Accordingly, when he was ready to sail, he sought out his friend Friar Juan Perez, who heard his confession and gave him communion. This devout example was followed by the rest of his men, who still felt forebodings over the dangers of the unknown sea and the need for comfort and protection of the Almighty.

The Admiral's little fleet sailed from Palos a half hour before sunrise on August 3, 1492. Many of the men believed that they had seen Spain for the last time.

PART II

First Voyage

CHAPTER 5

HISTORIC CROSSING

THE first voyage of Columbus was the greatest voyage of discovery ever made. Its successful completion was a singular tribute to the discoverer's stubborn determination and skill. During the western passage he overcame the threats of capture, ship damage, fear, superstition, doubt, and near mutiny. On the return trip he survived one of the roughest winters ever recorded in the stormy Atlantic, and brought the *Niña* through tremendous seas into safe harbor as admiring fishermen watched from the cliffs of the Portuguese coast.

When his fleet departed from Palos in August, the crews of the three ships regarded their commander as a meddlesome foreigner who had cast a spell over the rulers of Spain to obtain support for a mad adventure. But by the time *Niña* anchored in the Tagus River six months later, these same rough, ignorant sailors knew him to be a master mariner whose skill at navigation and seamanship had saved the life of every man aboard.

Columbus was a man with a mission. By some intuitive reasoning, he sensed the importance of his enterprise and its impact on history. To make sure that it would be properly recorded for posterity, he decided to keep a journal, which he opened with a sonorous (and somewhat pompous) preamble summarizing the circumstances and purpose of the enterprise:

"In the name of Jesus Christ.

"Most high, most Christian, most excellent and most powerful princes, our lord the King, and our sovereign the Queen, of the Spains and of the islands of the sea, this present year 1492:

"As Your Highnesses had ended the war against the Moors ruling in Europe, which was terminated at the great city of Granada, where, on the 12th of January, in this year, I saw the royal standards of your Highnesses, by force of arms, hung on the towers of the Alhambra . . . presently in the same month, Your Highnesses . . . thought of sending me, Christopher Columbus, to the aforesaid countries of India . . . to observe their disposition and the means and method that could be used . . . you directed me . . . to take . . . the way of the west, by which we have no positive knowledge that any one has ever passed until now . . . For this purpose you bestowed many favors and conferred nobility on me . . . and decreed that my eldest son should be my successor, and so on from generation to generation for ever . . .

"I armed three vessels well adapted for such service, and spread sail from that port [Palos] well supplied with provisions and pilots . . . and followed the course of the Canary Islands . . .

*to sail from there until I should reach the Indies
. . . and accomplish all your Highnesses charged
me with.*

*"I propose . . . to describe this voyage most
carefully, and to record day by day all I shall do and
see, and that shall happen to me . . . I intend
making a new marine chart, on which I shall set
down all the waters and the lands of the Ocean
sea in their proper places . . . and I mean to compose a book in which I shall represent the whole
as in a picture, by latitude from the equanoctial
line, and longitude from the West.*

*"Above all, it is of utmost importance that I
should shun sleep, and study my navigation per-
severingly, to fulfill all duties laid on me, which will
be a great labor."*

Shaping his course to the southwest, Columbus stood
for the Canary Islands, which lie about 150 miles off
the west coast of Africa. During this leg he demonstrated his superiority at navigation, making a landfall
on August 9 when all of his pilots insisted that there was
still considerable distance to go. He had hoped to spend
only a few days there in order to top off supplies, but
a serious problem on the *Pinta* dragged out the total
delay to about a month. On the third day out of Palos,
Martín Alonzo Pinzón signaled that the *Pinta*'s rudder
was broken. Columbus suspected sabotage by the reluctant shipowners back in Palos. The capable Pinzón soon
made a makeshift jury rig which lasted a while, but the
rudder continued to give trouble, and on top of that,
the *Pinta* began to leak. With that, Columbus determined to find another ship to commandeer in her place.

Unfavorable wind and weather stalled him for two days, but on the 12th of August he put in to Gomera, directing Martín Alonzo to make for Las Palmas. He waited for eleven days, daily expecting another Spanish ship, but finally gave up and crossed over to Las Palmas. There he found the *Pinta*, which had just arrived the day before; it had barely made port at all. Upon learning that the only ship suitable to replace the *Pinta* had departed a few days earlier, Columbus determined to make the necessary repairs to the caravel and continue. At the same time, he directed Vicente Pinzón to change the rig of the *Niña*. That ship's lateen sails were not as efficient as the square rigs of the *Santa Maria* and *Pinta*, especially for following the easterly winds that the Admiral anticipated on the outward voyage.

On September 2 the fleet of three ships, once again intact, sailed for Gomera to load provisions which three of the crew had been accumulating during *Santa Maria*'s absence. When they were ready for sea, the ships sailed back to Las Palmas, passing close to the volcano of Tenerife which was then in full eruption. The effect of this awesome sight struck terror in the hearts of the crew. Smoke and flames billowed skyward and red molten lava flowed down the mountainside. The men grew alarmed and afraid, thinking that this was another omen of bad luck, which, combined with *Pinta*'s misfortunes and other signs that the superstitious sailors regarded as ominous, was ample reason for turning back to Spain. Columbus reasoned with the crew as if they were frightened children, telling them how he had seen similar sights at Mount Etna, and calming them with descriptions of the gold and glory that lay ahead.

In Las Palmas they learned of yet another obstacle.

Three Portuguese men-of-war were lurking offshore to seize the Spanish ships. Doubtless King John resented Columbus' refusal to return to Portugal, and was determined to prevent a voyage that promised such riches to Spain. Columbus' only recourse was to evade them; he could not hope to pit his small ships against such odds. Accordingly, he put to sea immediately. This final departure, on September 6, also began poorly. His dash for freedom soon slowed to a walk, and then to a halt. The winds died and his ships lay becalmed. Finally, on Sunday morning, September 9, easterly winds set in and the fleet of caravels scudded over the horizon, leaving their pursuers—and their last sight of land—behind them.

The weather turned mild, and the wind blew consistently from the east. Columbus had chosen the longest route across the Atlantic; but it was ideal, for it was the perfect sailing route, possessing winds and currents that still wash European fishing floats ashore on Caribbean islands. Although Columbus had no way of knowing it, his delay in the Canaries had actually been fortunate. By a few weeks' margin he missed one of those seasonal typhoons that occur in the Caribbean at that season of the year.

Despite these delightful sailing conditions, the sailors lamented their fate. Some grizzled seamen broke down and wept; they would welcome the violence of the sea, they said, rather than face the unknown dangers that lay ahead. Modern readers who might have difficulty understanding the depth of such fear should relate it to the early space voyages of the twentieth century, and imagine the feelings of those who will be aboard the first spaceship to the moon.

They sailed west along the 28th parallel of north

latitude. Columbus' cruising instructions to the captains of the other ships required them to stay within sight of the *Santa Maria*. Should the ships become separated, they were to continue westward for seven hundred leagues (about 2,100 nautical miles), where the Admiral expected to find land. After crossing that distance they were instructed to proceed with caution, lie to at night for safety, and keep a careful lookout for rocks and shoals by day.

While he was fairly confident that his cruising plans were correct, Columbus used a canny stratagem to conceal from his men the true distance traveled. He needed a little leeway and margin for error to prevent panic among his men if his predictions turned out to be in error. Thus Columbus kept *two* records. In his private journal, which he hid from everyone, he recorded his best estimate of distance traveled. (Later study showed that he overestimated by about 9 per cent.) For public viewing and for inspection by the crew, he showed a reduced daily run. Thus when they had a day's run of 100 miles, he would show 80 miles. Actually, the distance made good was about halfway between his two records.

After several days' sailing, Columbus observed a phenomenon which could not be concealed from knowledgeable seamen. The compass needle no longer pointed toward the North Star. Each day it pointed a little more to the west of Polaris. What Columbus was encountering was a change in the earth's magnetic variation, something that no one had expected—it was unknown to science. Being more alert in his observations, he had a few days' grace in which to invent an explanation before his pilots noticed the change. When they became alarmed, the Admiral was ready with a logical (but quite erroneous) theory. The needle, he said, pointed to a fixed bearing in space, and the North Star revolved about it just as other stars in the universe did. Suspicion gave way to belief as the pilots deferred to the Admiral's superior knowledge. A few years later, Sebastian Cabot noticed this same movement during his voyages of discovery to the northeastern coasts of America. He used this characteristic of the compass needle to estimate longitude, and considered it a great secret, which, it is said, he related only on his deathbed.

By the 16th of September all hands were eagerly looking for signs of land. Suddenly they sighted what appeared to be a green meadow and there was premature rejoicing. Actually, they were on the edge of the Sargasso Sea, where acres of floating seaweed give this impression. At first they were cheered, thinking that the weed had broken off from nearby rocks and drifted out to sea. But they traveled through it for days, finding no bottom with the deep sea lead. They did notice, however, a live crab, a tunny fish, and certain birds in the area which supported their belief that land was nearby. Columbus knew that he had traveled only about half the distance required to find land, and refused to alter course on the basis of such unreliable evidence. So they continued west day after day, and the mutterings of the crew grew louder. Even the favorable wind became a source of alarm. How could they beat their way back—a long tedious process in a square rigger— before they ran out of food? It was madness, they thought, and each day's travel to the west made their problems seem greater.

Columbus noted how the men would gather into little

groups to discuss their fears. The dark scowls and whispered conferences were too obvious to overlook. Despite his reassurances, and the hope he exuded at each new bird, fish, or flotsam that indicated that land was nearby, his words lost their effectiveness through repetition. By September 22 the men were almost in open revolt, but their mood changed when the wind drifted to the west. This change slowed the ships, but it cheered the crews. Here, at last, was evidence of favorable wind for the return trip. Shortly thereafter a storm burst on them and for two days they expended all their energy tending the ship. On the 25th the seas became calm again, after which the easterly trades set in and pushed the ships westward at a rapid rate once more.

At this point, Martín Alonzo Pinzón was deceived by a heavy cloud bank on the horizon ahead and shouted "Land! Land!" The crews fell to their knees and loudly thanked God for their good fortune. All sang "Gloria in excelsis Deo," and joy replaced their earlier fears. By sunrise, however, everyone realized that it had been a false alarm. Once more the dejected crews turned to discussions of home, of the great risks that lay ahead, and the madness of their leader. Still they sailed westward as Columbus stubbornly hung on to his conviction. Daily they saw fresh signs of land. There were fish of species that never strayed far from shore, small birds in increasing numbers, branches of trees, and fresh stalks with fruit still on them. Alternately encouraged and disappointed, they looked at the determined figure of Columbus, and hoped daily for a sign of indecision. None came. They continued west as before until October 7, when the *Niña*, which was in the lead, hoisted a signal flag and fired a gun to announce discovery of land.

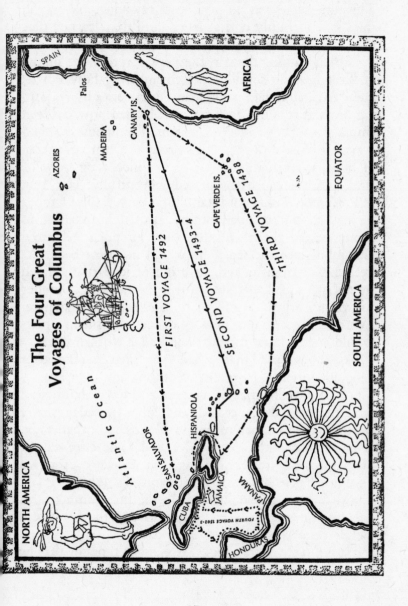

The Four Great Voyages of Columbus

This time there was no premature rejoicing, and so the ships sailed steadily on in silence until they learned that this, too, had been a mirage.

In their ensuing despair, they saw several large flights of birds heading southwest. Remembering how Portuguese navigators had made many discoveries by following birds at sea, and realizing that he had now covered ample distance to reach Cipangu, Columbus changed course to the southwest. This brought a temporary ray of hope, more flights of birds, and increasing signs of land. But three more days passed uneventfully. The crew of the *Santa Maria* could stand it no longer. On October 10 they considered open mutiny. A small but vociferous group passed the word that they intended to throw Columbus into the sea if he would not turn back. As before, Columbus talked them out of it, partially aided by a sharp squall that swept over the horizon. October 11 was a critical day. Signs of land were everywhere. Were it not for this new evidence, the sullen crews would surely have forced their leader to turn back.

Columbus sensed that he had won. That evening, after religious services, he gathered officers and men around him and gave them a stirring talk. They would sight land the next day, he said, and he promised a velvet jacket to the first man to find it. No one slept that night. They crowded the ships' sides, and some climbed the rigging for a better view. King Ferdinand had promised an annual pension of 10,000 maravedis (about $750) to the first man to sight land. In the fifteenth century, this amount was sufficient to take care of the needs of a simple seaman for the rest of his days.

At ten o'clock that night, Columbus thought that he saw a light on the horizon. It flickered and moved as if it were a small boat. He called Pedro Gutierrez and Rodrigo Sanchez to him to see if they could see it too. Gutierrez said that he saw it, but by the time Sanchez arrived on the poop deck it was gone. This was important confirmation, however, which stood in the Admiral's favor when the "first sighting" award was determined. Four hours later, at 2 A.M. on October 12, seaman Rodrigo de Triana of the *Pinta* sighted land. Martín Pinzón fired a signal gun to signify success, and all ships took in sail.

They had been making 12 knots due west under full sail and would surely have piled into the rocks off the eastern shore of the island if they had not taken this precaution. But Columbus was too experienced a seaman to let disaster ruin all of his efforts at this point. With sails trimmed the ships lay to, making "short-boards" as they slowly cruised back and forth over the same water.

These must have been the most anxious moments of the Admiral's career. After a lifetime of ridicule, his dreams were about to be realized. What would he find with the morning sun? Japan? China? The riches of the Indies? Unfortunately, none of these intense personal thoughts or expressions of joy were recorded in his journal. But it is easy to imagine the excitement that pervaded all ships as they waited for sunrise.

CHAPTER 6

ISLAND
DISCOVERIES

IT is one of the great disappointments of history that this first landfall of Columbus' was never positively identified. Scholars have traced and retraced Columbus' steps and have closely studied the description in his journal. The preponderance of evidence points to San Salvador, or Watling's Island, a flat bit of land in the Bahamas about 13 miles long and 6 miles wide. The first definitive work which answered most doubts and speculations was done by Lieutenant J. B. Murdoch, U.S. Navy, in 1884. Taking the courses, distances, and dates of Columbus' journal, he plotted the track backward from Cuba, and ended at Watling's Island, at latitude 24° N., longitude 74°30′ W.

At dawn Columbus saw a green tropical island, lush with foliage and inhabited by naked natives. He took his ships to the western side of it and anchored in a cove that was clear of coral reefs. Shortly thereafter, each ship lowered a boat to send its captain and official party ashore. With banners waving in the breeze and with appropriate pomp and ceremony this band of men made the famed "landing of Columbus."

They gave devout thanks to God for a safe passage and formally claimed the land for Spain in the name of King Ferdinand and Queen Isabella. The court secretary, Rodrigo de Escobedo, duly recorded and notarized the proceedings, entering the Admiral's name for the island, San Salvador, into the record.

The party then turned their attention to the natives, who were curious but afraid. Columbus' son Ferdinand wrote that "the Admiral, perceiving they were a gentle, peaceful, and very simple people, gave them little red caps and glass beads which they hung around their necks, together with other trifles that they cherished as if they were precious stones of great price."

In his letter to the Spanish court describing his first voyage, Columbus wrote that "they bartered like idiots, cotton and gold for fragments of bows, glasses, bottles and jars." He also noticed that they had "a firm belief that . . . all good things are in heaven, and that I descended from thence with these ships and sailors, and under this impression I was received after they had thrown aside their fears. Nor are they slow or stupid, but of clear understanding . . . but they never saw any people clothed, nor any ships like ours."

Believing that he was on an island near the eastern end of India, Columbus called these natives "Indians." The name was generally used in Europe before the true nature of the New World became evident. By that time the natives of both North America and South America were habitually called Indians and the name stuck.

The results of this landing were far-reaching. It highlighted the contrast between the old world and the new, and marked the beginning of modern history. Columbus had demonstrated by actual experiment that the earth was not flat and that land could be reached by sailing west. Medieval Europe emerged from its cocoon and the era of the "whole world" began. Columbus' theories to the contrary, history has shown that it was much more important to the human race that he discovered America than it would have been had he found a new ocean route to India.

Understandably, the search for gold obsessed everyone on the shore of San Salvador. Columbus had used the promise of riches to hold his frightened and discontented crews together during the dark days of their transit. Now that he had found land, it was important that he make this promise good. Perceiving bits of gold ornaments dangling from the nose and ears of some of the natives, Columbus inquired, by sign language, where the gold had come from. They pointed to the south and west. Thus they innocently established the direction of exploration for the remainder of the voyage.

Two days were sufficient to satisfy all hands that San Salvador had very little to offer. Taking some hostages to act as guides and interpreters, Columbus sailed on October 14. The remainder of his voyage can by divided roughly into three parts: cruising the Bahamas; exploring Cuba; and coasting the shores of Haiti.

The cruise through the Bahamas yielded little gold, but Columbus and his men were overcome by the beauty of these sunny islands. From the beginning, Columbus showed the prudence and skill of a master seaman. As the first white man to sail these waters, he had to rely on soundings and "eyeball navigation" alone. Since that time, literally hundreds of ships have come to grief in the Caribbean passages, even though they are well surveyed. Navy charts today are dotted with small crosses to mark the wrecks of less fortunate and less capable mariners. Columbus noted that the water was usually quite deep and clear right up to the shoreline, but there he had to keep a sharp eye out for rocks under water. As a rule he would lie to at night, and choose his anchorage carefully well offshore lest he foul his anchor among the rocks. The loss of irreplaceable anchors at this remote distance from civilization would have been a calamity indeed.

In his journal, Columbus noted that he had many islands to choose from as his next call after San Salvador. Accordingly he "looked for the biggest" and set sail. In succession he coasted and named the following islands:

October 15—Santa Maria de la Concepción (Rum Cay)
October 17—Fernandina (Long Island)
October 19—Isabella (Crooked Island)
October 25—Islas de Arena (Ragged Island)

Historians have noted the logic of his names. Deeply religious, Columbus named the first after the Blessed Saviour and the second for the Virgin Mary. The next two were named for his sovereigns, Ferdinand and Isabella. Later on he honored friends and family, but generally he seemed to use names that were symbolic of the circumstances or the moment.

Ashore in Santa Maria de la Concepción, Columbus found crowds of friendly natives who were willing to trade cotton and small artifacts, but none had any significant amount of gold. At Fernandina his men entered native houses and discovered "swinging beds" called "hamacs," which were quickly adopted by sailors as the most comfortable bunks that ever sailed the seas.

Anchored off Isabella, Columbus learned of a king "who goes clothed and wears much gold." For several days he searched in vain for this mysterious dignitary, but to no avail. He did, however, notice different barks and leaves which he believed would yield spices. And on Isabella the men killed an iguana, which they described as a "large serpent." Disappointed in his swing through these lesser islands, Columbus sailed at midnight on October 24 for Cuba, an island described by natives as one that teemed with ships, large cities, and gold and spices in great abundance. This, Columbus thought, must be Marco Polo's island of Cipangu (Japan), where he would meet the Great Khan and load his ships to the gunwales with fabulous cargo.

Arriving at Cuba on the 28th, the ships entered a deep river and anchored. This landfall is also disputed, but it is believed to be Bahia Bariay, which lies on the north coast of the eastern part of Cuba (in Oriente Province). Columbus noted that the mountains of Cuba were like those of Sicily, and he was enchanted with the beauty of his surroundings. His native guides informed him that the island had 10 great rivers entering the sea, and that it was so large that it required more than 20 days to circumnavigate it in a canoe. Exploration of the coast produced little that they had not seen on the smaller islands to the north. They did note domesticated birds, dogs that could not bark, and statues of women in some of the huts. From native stories of a great ruler in a distant city, Columbus concluded that he had found the coast of Cathay and that he should send out an expeditionary party in search of the Great Khan.

He chose Luis de Torres, the former Jew, now a trusted interpreter, who was accompanied by Rodrigo de Xerez and two Indians. He instructed these representatives to pay his respects to the monarch and to inform him that they had been sent by the great rulers of Spain to establish friendly relations between their countries. Columbus also wished to learn certain geographical facts about the coastline that he had discovered, as well as any information they could obtain on the production of drugs and spices.

While his mission to the Khan was traveling overland, Columbus beached his ships one at a time in order to clean and scrape their bottoms. Only three months had elapsed since they sailed from Palos, but the dread teredo, or sea worm, was particularly active in warm water. Columbus maintained good discipline over his men, encouraging them to search the surrounding country for specimens of flora and minerals which might prove valuable. Next to his great obsession, gold and precious stones, he hoped to find spices and drugs. Two of his discoveries in Cuba turned out to be quite important to mankind. These were the sweet potato, or yam, and tobacco. Luis de Torres and Rodrigo de Xerez were the first to see natives "drinking" tobacco, and described it as follows:

> *"The men carried in their hand a burning coal, and certain weeds for inhaling their smoke. These were dry weeds rolled up in a leaf, which was dry also, shaped like the paper muskets the boys make on the feast of Pentecost, and lighting one end of it, they suck the other, and absorb or inhale the smoke, whereby they are put to sleep and made almost drunk, and in this way they do not feel fatigue."*

Las Casas, writing 40 years later, noted that some Spaniards in Hispaniola who had acquired the habit, when told that it was injurious, had replied that they "could not give it up." Since that time, tobacco has been one of the greatest sources of revenue obtained from the Caribbean.

The inland "ambassadors" returned on the night of November 5. Their report was so negative that Columbus determined to quit Cuba and to continue his search for gold. Torres and Xerez had traveled about 40 miles into the interior to find a village of 50 houses. Here they were received warmly, and were worshiped as men from heaven. However, all that they had seen throughout their journey was the same poverty and lower forms of civilization that existed in villages on the coast.

Once more ready for sea, the three ships sailed on November 12. Columbus ordered his crew to seize several young native men and women as hostages. He explained that he wanted to train the men to be interpreters, and that he brought women along to keep the Indian men contented. Later he was roundly criticized by churchmen of Spain for having carried off women who had their own husbands, and subjecting them to the pleasures of other men.

Encountering unfavorable winds, the ships made little headway to the east. In two days they barely covered 60 miles. Sensing that a storm was about to break as the wind shifted northeast, Columbus sought shelter in a safe harbor. He doubled back and entered Tanamo Bay (which he named Our Lady's Sea), one of the most scenic bays on the island of Cuba. It is studded with beautiful wooded islets that rise right up out of the water to heights of up to 250 feet. In his descriptions

Columbus waxed poetic and leaned toward exaggeration, but it is plainly evident that he enjoyed this haven, and was reluctant to leave. He coasted around the bay in the ship's boat, threading a passage between the islets and marveling at their thick green slopes. On Sunday, the 18th, he took a large party with him to Porto Principe, the first harbor at the bay's entrance, and officially claimed the land for Spain. Following his usual custom, he instructed his carpenters to make a huge cross near the entrance, which Ferdinand Columbus described as "very tall and very fine to look upon."

Five days was all that he could spare in idleness; there was work to do and gold to discover. Once again he sailed at sunrise in search of islands to the east, where, according to the natives, gold was gathered on the beaches at night by torchlight. The easterly trades were against him all day Monday, so his course made good was to the northeast toward Isabella. Having some natives on board from that island, Columbus put about before he came close to land so they would not be tempted to escape and swim home. Unable to make Tanamo Bay because of adverse winds and current, the Admiral kept at sea and doggedly tried to make headway. He was unsuccessful until the evening of November 21, when a change in the wind made an easterly transit feasible. This was a short-lived blessing, and soon thereafter Columbus decided to steer south for Cuba once more. At this point, Martín Alonzo Pinzón rebelled and took the *Pinta* over the horizon to the east, where an Indian had told him the island of Babeque (Great Inagua) lay. Pinzón was dazzled by the reports of gold on Babeque and was determined to get there first.

Now Columbus was down to two ships. He anchored

about 25 miles to the east of Tanamo Bay on November 24, and waited for a shift of wind. During this layover he toured about in the small boat, and once more was greatly impressed by the scenery. For ten more days he alternately sailed east and anchored, clawing his way against the current whenever the wind was slightly favorable. One of his anchorages was Porto Santo, whose natural advantages were so obvious that it became the site of the first Spanish settlement in Cuba 20 years later. By the 5th of December the ships had reached the eastern point of Cuba where the coast tends southwest. The natives aboard begged Columbus to leave this part of the island immediately. The coast of Oriente, they feared, was the land of the fierce Carib Indians, who ate their captives.

Entering Windward Passage, which separates Cuba from Haiti, Columbus saw the mountains of Haiti to the east. Babeque, the fabled island of gold, lay to the northeast, forcing him to make a choice. However, the wind shifted to the northeast and it was impossible for the caravels to sail toward Babeque. Steering east-south-east, he arrived off the coast of Haiti at dusk, where he tacked back and forth over good water until daylight the next morning, when he was able to find a safe entrance.

On December 6, the ships were anchored in a fine harbor near the western tip of Haiti. Columbus named it Port St. Nicholas in honor of a church feast day that coincided with their arrival. Here the natives fled from them and determinedly resisted all contact with the strangers. Accordingly, Columbus moved on, catching a favorable wind off the entrance of Port St. Nicholas and making good time eastward until another impending storm sent him shoreward in search of an anchorage. He put in to a large bay, naming it Porto Conceptión, and was held there a week by unfavorable winds. The weather, the scenery, the birds, and even the fish in the harbor reminded everyone so much of home that Columbus named the island "Hispaniola."

Three sailors encountered a number of natives in the woods on December 12 and managed to capture "a young and beautiful savage" whom they brought to the Admiral. She was entirely naked, but her physical attractions were outshone by a golden ornament that she wore in her nose. The Spanish treated her well, gave her clothing and presents, and set her ashore. She departed reluctantly, protesting that she would prefer to remain on the ship, but Columbus needed to make contact with island inhabitants and hoped that she would provide the means. The next day an expedition from the ships found a village of 2,000 natives and established good relations with them. This delightful spot was fertile and attractive, but there was no gold to be found anywhere.

A few miles to the north, there is a channel between the island of Tortuga and the Haitian coast. Columbus put to sea on December 14 and tacked his way eastward through the channel. On the 16th he landed at Porto Paz (Port de Paix) for more successful negotiations with the natives. This time there was more evidence of gold and trade was brisk. A young chieftain came aboard to visit and exchange gifts. Although he was naked, he made an impressive appearance, as did a higher chieftain, or cacique, who came aboard with even more pomp and ceremony on the 18th. This visit was best decribed by Columbus himself, who wrote:

"Your Highnesses would doubtless think well of the dignity and respect in which they hold him, though they all go naked. When he came aboard, he found me dining at the table below the stern-castle, and quickly came to seat himself beside me; nor would he let me rise to meet him or get up from the table, but insisted that I should eat. And when he entered below the castle, he signalled with his hand that all his people should remain outside, and they did this with the greatest readiness and respect in the world, and they all seated themselves on the deck, except two men of ripe years whom I took to be his councilors and tutors, who sat at his feet . . .

"After dinner his squire brought a belt like those of Castile in shape, but of different workmanship, which he gave to me, and two pieces of worked gold which were very thin, so that I believe they obtain little gold here, though I think they are very near to where it comes from and that there is much of it."

After exchanging presents, Columbus set the young cacique ashore with full side honors and a few gun salvos. While his trading had netted only a small amount of gold, he had received a treasure of information from one of the cacique's elder councilors. Gold lay to the east.

Columbus was under way that night with the land breeze, and managed to work his way east to Porto St. Thomas by December 20. In this comfortable snug harbor (now called Acul Bay) he carried out a brisk but unspectacular trade for three days. A messenger arrived with an invitation to visit the grand cacique Guacanagari who lived farther to the east. As persuasion the chief sent a valuable mask of beads, feathers, bones, and wood, ornamented with gold. Unable to get his ships clear because of the wind, the Admiral sent a ship's boat with a representative party. They were received with such great courtesy and generosity that they returned to urge Columbus to hasten his visit. He got under way the next day, December 24, with all hands enjoying the prospect of a pleasant Christmas Day with Guacanagari's people.

Here, for the only time in his many years at sea, Columbus was guilty of an unseamanlike practice. It was usually his custom to stay on deck at all times in threatening weather or when piloting unknown waters. This night, however, he turned in, relying on a report from the boat that visited Guacanagari's village that the route was safe. No sooner did he turn in than the helmsman decided to catch a few winks himself. He turned the tiller over to the boy who was "grommet" of the watch, a practice that the Admiral had forbidden. The young and inexperienced lad promptly allowed the current to push *Santa María* off course and onto a reef. By the time his shouts had aroused the sleepy crew, the flagship was hard aground with an ebbing tide. The first on deck, Columbus took in the situation quickly and ordered the master, Juan de la Cosa, to carry out an anchor astern in the ship's boat for a purchase that might pull the *Santa Maria* free. This action could have saved the ship, but Juan de la Cosa ignored the orders and headed for *Niña* and safety. This cowardly act proved to be the doom of *Santa Maria*. She piled higher and higher onto the reef with each succeeding swell. Soon her seams opened and water poured into the hold. Columbus ordered the mainmast cut away to lighten the ship, but even this desperate measure failed. As the ship slowly pounded itself to pieces, the *Santa Maria*'s boat returned, accompanied by *Niña*'s master in his own boat. Fortunately there was time to abandon ship before it completely broke up, so the entire crew was able to transfer to *Niña* without any loss of life. It was a sad day for Columbus, and it was, incidentally, the only ship that he ever lost by shipwreck in all of his voyages into these unknown waters.

The next day, which was Christmas Day, the men made frequent trips to the groaning *Santa Maria* to salvage her cargo. The native chief, the cacique Guacanagari, provided a great many boats to assist in this, and the job was done quickly. To the cacique's great credit he established an armed guard over the cargo and cared for the goods so diligently that not a piece was stolen. He sent relatives to console the grieving Admiral aboard *Niña*, and when he saw how a few gifts of gold cheered the great mariner, he promised much more. So hospitable was this chieftain and so friendly were his people that it seemed only natural for Columbus to decide to leave part of his expedition there to establish a settlement. Actually there was little other choice, for the tiny *Niña* would have been hard put to accommodate all of *Santa Maria*'s crew on the return voyage.

There was no dearth of volunteers for the settlement. The vision of pleasant living among hospitable natives not far from the island's source of gold was a lure that few could resist. With characteristic energy, Columbus set about building a fortress which he named La Navidad in honor of the Nativity, and gradually he came to look upon the loss of his ship as a providential act which would lead him to even greater riches and glory. Salvaged planks and equipment from *Santa Maria* soon were fitted together to form this first European outpost in the Caribbean. Forty men volunteered to remain behind. Columbus put Diego de Harana in charge, and made preparations to leave.

On the 27th of December he learned that the *Pinta* was anchored in a harbor near the eastern end of the island. This was good news indeed, for each ship needed the other as insurance against the dangers of sailing into unknown waters. Columbus hastened his preparations, and on January 4, after a great day of feasting with Guacanagari, he departed. The *Pinta* and *Niña* rendezvoused on the 6th, permitting a meeting of the two captains. Martín Alonzo Pinzón produced an unlikely story of his wanderings, which Columbus accepted at face value, more because of necessity than belief. The two ships sailed east to Porto Blanca, where *Pinta* had spent three weeks, paused for two days, and then continued on to Cape Samana.

The two small vessels anchored in a small bay that Columbus named Bahia de las Flechas (Bay of Arrows) in honor of an incident that took place with the natives there. These Indians were a different cut from those the men had encountered earlier. They were fierce looking and independent. During an argument that arose over trading, the Indians made a threatening move toward their bows and arrows, which they had stacked in a pile while trade was carried on. The hardy Spaniards set upon them so promptly and fiercely that only seven of them put 55 Indians into headlong flight. A local cacique came to make peace the next day, presenting his gold crown to Columbus as a token of good faith. At length, on January 16, the Admiral bade final good-bye to the island and started out on the return voyage, with both of the heavily laden ships leaking more than he would have liked.

CHAPTER 7

TRIUMPHANT RETURN

DURING the westward crossing from Spain to the Caribbean, the crews of the *Santa Maria, Pinta,* and *Niña* had spent many hours in idle speculation about their return trip. How could these square-rigged, round-bottomed ships make headway against the trades that always blew from the east? This now became Columbus' problem to solve. How should he steer a homeward course? He knew that Spain was vaguely to the northeast; however, when he left Hispaniola, he had to take the east wind on the starboard tack. His resulting course was a little east of north, but that was the best he could do. For several days the two ships worked northward, changing direction only when the Admiral ventured a port tack; then he found himself heading east-southeast, toward Africa. For several days the ships cruised on a northerly heading, until they reached the approximate latitude of Bermuda. Then the wind backed around and suddenly Columbus found that he was in the midst of the westerlies that were fair for an easterly heading and home.

It was winter, one of the roughest in the history of the stormy Atlantic. The winds turned icy, plaguing the barefoot sailors and driving them to shelter. Gale winds sprinkled with sleet pounded against the caravel's rigging, wearing out sails, ropes, and men. Through it all, Columbus was almost constantly on deck.

In a shouting conference with the *Pinta,* the pilots of the two vessels found that neither agreed with the other as to their location. Some thought that they were near the latitude of the Madeiras, and others thought that they were headed straight for Gibraltar. Columbus' chart showed that they were closer to the Azores. As usual, he was right.

By the 12th of February, the ships had begun to labor heavily in a rough sea. The weather grew steadily worse, and on the 14th it was so bad that even an experienced mariner like Columbus called the waves "frightful." He summoned the crew to draw lots for a pilgrimage of penance once they reached land. Amidst the fury of the storm, the men put as many peas into a cap as there were sailors on board; one of the peas was marked with a cross. Whoever drew this pea would make a pilgrimage to Santa Maria de Guadalupe, carrying a five-pound candle. The Admiral was the first to draw, and the lot fell on him. Another pilgrimage, to Santa Maria de Loretto, fell to seaman Pedro de Villa; and a third lot, to say mass at Santa Clara de Moguer, again fell to the Admiral.

While *Niña* labored in a cross sea that frequently broke over her, Columbus ordered his men to fill empty wine and water casks with seawater and stow them below as ballast. This gave the ship more stability and the contained liquid prevented a free surface effect—a dangerous phenomenon caused by the unchecked movement of water in a ship's hold.

The fury of the storm continued, separating *Niña* from *Pinta* during the night and for the remainder of the voyage. In his journal Columbus noted that his greatest worry was for his two sons, Diego and Ferdinand, who would be left fatherless in a strange country if his ship went down. It was this fear, and the gnawing realization that his great story would never be told, that caused him to write a brief summary and set it afloat (as described in the preface to this book).

During the morning of the 15th, land was sighted to the northeast. This landfall was as welcome as the sighting of San Salvador had been four months earlier. There were various opinions as to its identity. One pilot thought that it was Madeira, another called it the Rock of Cintra, near Lisbon, and others thought that they were looking at their beloved coast of Spain. Columbus maintained that it was an island of the Azores. After two days' laboring against the wind and sea he finally brought *Niña* to anchor, and learned that he was indeed at Santa Clara, a small island of the Azores group about forty miles south of San Miguel.

For the first time in several days, the weary Admiral was able to get some sleep. He complained of pains in his legs caused by the wet and cold hours of his vigil through the storm. This was a form of arthritis and it remained with him the rest of his life, a painful testimonial to the rigors of his profession.

Niña remained in the Azores for seven days. During this time the hostile governor of Santa Clara endeavored to capture the entire crew by deception. It was not enough to have completed a terrifying and demanding voyage; now Columbus had to live by his wits to avoid a new disaster. He sent half of his crew ashore to say prayers of thanksgiving at a nearby church. En route they were seized by an armed guard and made prisoners. Suspecting chicanery, Columbus got his ship under way and issued arms to the few seamen, boys, and Indians who had remained. The governor approached within hailing distance of *Niña* in the ship's boat, but refused an invitation to board. At this distance he and Columbus exchanged heated views and warnings. Columbus sailed north for San Miguel, but was turned back by fog and weather. Upon his return to Santa Clara an embassy of three islanders came aboard to verify the orders under which Columbus sailed. Satisfied by the patent from Castile, they went ashore and released the Spanish prisoners. This uncivil reception could have ended in ignominious capture but for Columbus' alert action and persuasive tongue.

Two days later, on the 24th of February, *Niña* headed east for Spain with a favorable wind. After two days of good sailing they reached the edges of a winter gale that was worse than the storm that they had weathered west of the Azores. This storm moved eastward, right along the caravel's track, building up to a climax on March 3, when a sudden gust of wind split her sails. Waves tossed the ship high in the air and then dashed against her from both sides. The scene was so terrifying that the men once more resorted to drawing lots for a pilgrimage. Again Columbus drew the pea marked with a cross. Some historians have read mystic meanings into the Admiral's persistent winning of the right of pilgrimage; no doubt Columbus did, too. The entire crew vowed to fast on bread and water the first Saturday ashore if their lives were spared.

Perhaps with divine guidance, and certainly with Columbus' superb seamanship, *Niña* rode out the storm and barely escaped shipwreck off the rugged coast of Portugal. With his last remaining sail from the sail locker, Columbus clawed his way to safety, and entered the haven of the Tagus River on March 4. Upon anchoring at Belem, a small fishing village near the river's mouth, local seamen informed him that they had never seen such a stormy winter season. Many ships had been held in the harbor for four months by contrary weather, and twenty-five vessels had been wrecked on the coast of Flanders.

The news of *Niña*'s great voyage spread quickly throughout Lisbon. Soon every barge and boat of the city clustered around the weathered caravel, and hundreds of visitors boarded to gaze upon the Indians and to hear the proud sailors tell of their adventures. On the 8th of March a Portuguese noble arrived with an invitation for Columbus to visit King John at Valparaiso, where he was then holding court. Columbus was hesitant at first, but soon agreed to go. After all, he was completely at the mercy of the Portuguese monarch. King John received him with great ceremony and permitted the Admiral to be seated in his presence—a courtesy usually granted only to royalty.

The king asked many detailed questions about the voyage, the islands, the soil, the people, and the weather. Columbus talked enthusiastically and with such energy that many members of the court thought that he was being boastful. Some even went so far as to suggest his assassination.

King John would have none of it, and graciously sent Columbus back to Lisbon with an honorable escort. By the 13th of March, the weather had moderated enough for Columbus to take *Niña* to sea. Two days later he received a tumultuous welcome at Palos. To the seafaring folk of this town, the full meaning of the great voyage was readily apparent. Besides, their men were returning from what they had considered certain death seven months before. It was an occasion for feasting and celebration and for earnest prayers of thanksgiving.

Scarcely had the *Niña*'s reception begun when *Pinta* also entered the harbor, bringing more sailors safely back to their homes and loved ones. This arrival pleased everyone but *Pinta*'s commander, Martín Alonzo Pinzón, who had reason to avoid Columbus. *Pinta* had actually reached Spain before *Niña*, putting in to the Bay of Biscay at Bayonne while the former was at the Azores. Pinzón had doubted that *Niña* would survive the storm and consequently had hastened to inform Ferdinand and Isabella of his return. He requested permission to come to court and relate "his" discoveries. The sovereigns wisely refused, preferring to wait for the arrival of Columbus. This just rebuff, it is said, caused Pinzón such disappointment that he took to his bed and died of anguish and a broken heart. At any rate he died shortly afterward, having almost negated, by several questionable actions during the voyage, the great support he had given Columbus during the summer of 1492.

The famous "Letter of the First Voyage" which Columbus had dispatched to the sovereigns from Lisbon had caused great excitement in the Spanish court. The magnificence of this discovery, coming so soon after the Spanish victory at Granada, was viewed as a reward for the piety of Ferdinand and Isabella. These practical rulers were delighted with their new acquisition, but they nevertheless realized the importance of establishing their claim firmly in the community of nations. Even while they were preparing to receive Columbus with the highest honors, they were likewise planning another, larger expedition.

The period of spring and summer, 1493, was the zenith of Columbus' career. Everywhere he went he was acclaimed and honored. His procession to Barcelona passed through streets lined with eager spectators who stared in awe at the painted Indians, the parrots, the stuffed animals, and other artifacts from the Caribbean. With a flair for showmanship that is somewhat surprising, the dignified explorer organized his return procession somewhat like those of the Roman generals of old, whose triumphant entries into Rome were masterpieces of grandeur.

Ferdinand and Isabella, surrounded by all the dignitaries of their court, received their "Admiral of the Oceans" with the highest of honors. They listened eagerly as he recounted the glories of their new empire, and concluded the ceremony with fervent prayers.

The fame of Columbus spread beyond the Spanish border. His first letter-report was sent to Rome, where it was translated and printed in Latin. The demand was so great that it was printed over and over again, and was copied throughout the capitals of Europe. To match his growing fame the Spanish crown granted him a coat of arms, confirmed all of his titles, and awarded him the prize for being the first to sight land during the western passage. This last award was based on the testimony of the witnesses whom Columbus had called when he saw a light during the night of October 11.

King John of Portugal began preparations to send his own expedition to "the Indies." This alarmed Ferdinand and Isabella, who immediately set out to nail down the Spanish claim firmly for posterity. Already preparations for a second voyage were under way, and their famous Admiral of the Oceans was more than willing to lead the expedition. After all, he had left 40 good men at Haiti and they needed relief. Besides, there were several matters of unfinished business—such as finding Japan—that he wished to see to completion.

PART III

Second Voyage

CHAPTER 8

THE FLEET

AN able diplomat such as Ferdinand would not rely entirely on another voyage to solidify his claim to new lands and peoples. As soon as the Portuguese activity came to his attention, he appealed to Pope Alexander VI, who, in that day, was accepted by Christian nations as the international arbiter in matters of this kind. The Pope was a native of Spain who owed his election, it is said, to Ferdinand and Isabella. At any rate, he lent a sympathetic ear and issued several papal bulls, or decrees, dividing the oceans and lands between Portugal and Spain. The most important of these drew a line from north to south 100 leagues (318 miles) west of the Azores. All lands discovered to the east of this line were to belong to Portugal, and lands to the west would go to Spain. King John of Portugal continued to dissent, however, so the two kingdoms drew up a treaty which moved the line of demarcation almost 1,200 miles west of the Cape Verde Islands. This change eventually led to Portugal's claim to Brazil, but it gave to Spain the rest of the New World.

The Spanish sovereigns' detailed instructions for the second voyage emphasized their desire to convert the natives to the Catholic faith. Charging the Admiral to "treat the said Indians very well and lovingly, and abstain from doing them any injury," they provided men of the Church to teach the principles of the holy faith. These lengthy instructions also included details for fitting out the fleet, administering the men, and establishing a trading settlement in the islands. There was no doubt about the identity of the expedition's leader—Columbus was made captain-general of the fleet and his position as viceroy and governor of the islands was reaffirmed.

In contrast to the first voyage, which was minimally equipped, the second expedition was a veritable armada of supplies, men, and equipment that had had no equal in history. Fifteen hundred men and animals (pigs, sheep, goats, and fowl) for colonizing were crowded into the ships. Don Juan de Fonseca of Seville was in charge of preparations. While Columbus was at court, or traveling through the country making his pilgrimages, Don Juan gathered seventeen ships together and prepared them for the voyage. Lured by Columbus' fame and the prospect of adventure and wealth, so many men volunteered that it was difficult to choose who should go. When the ships actually sailed, several stowaways were discovered—doubtless the first such occurrence in a transatlantic crossing.

Among the 1,500 men there were about 300 who manned the ships. Another 200 were either cavaliers or hidalgos from wealthy families who took care of their own costs. The remainder were colonists, who signed on in the service of their king. These included farmers, artificers, doctors, and merchants. Columbus' younger brother, Diego, came from Genoa in time for the departure and was welcomed by the Admiral. Juan Ponce de León, who later discovered Florida, Juan de la Cosa, the mapmaker, and Dr. Chanca, a physician from Seville, were also in the group.

Ferdinand and his elder brother Diego looked on from the quays of Cádiz as the seventeen-ship squadron got under way. Three large "capital" ships lumbered along accompanied by smaller square-rigged caravels. *Niña* of first voyage fame, proudly followed the flagship *Santa Maria*, so named in honor of the flagship that had been wrecked on the reef at Cap Haitien. *Santa Maria* was nicknamed "Mariegalante," probably from the way she sailed, and her name was immortalized when the Admiral named one of the Leeward Islands in her honor. Two shallow-draft, lateen-rigged caravels were taken for river and coastal exploration.

One of the best sources for details of this voyage is the report of Doctor Chanca to the Chapter of Seville. This well-written, lively account is particularly valuable since it gives a third person's observations of the great mariner at sea. It was no mean feat to shepherd this motley group of ships, men, and beasts across the ocean. While Columbus had made one successful round trip to the Caribbean, there was no assurance that this second voyage would be equally successful. There were still a number of dangers and an uncharted ocean ahead of them. Any seaman who has sailed with a convoy will readily acknowledge the difficulties of keeping "closed up" and in station even in the days of steam. This group of strange ships, commanded by sailing captains of varying experiences and abilities, was held together by the skill and determination of Columbus, who truly earned his title "Admiral of the Oceans" on this voyage.

Sailing on Wednesday, September 25, 1493, the ships headed for the Canaries and favorable easterly trades. They arrived at Las Palmas on October 2 and anchored in Gomera on October 5. "We had to remain at Gomera," wrote Dr. Chanca, "to lay in our stores of meat, wood, and as much water as we could stow, preparatory to the long voyage which we expected to make without seeing land." Contrary winds and calm slowed their departure. After about a week of dawdling within sight of the islands, they finally caught a favorable wind and took departure from Ferro on October 13.

The route of the second voyage was more southerly than the first. This track took the fleet south of the Sargasso Sea in the direction of Guadeloupe in the chain of Leeward Islands. The crossing was uneventful, with the exception of one thunderstorm and the appearance of St. Elmo's fire in the rigging. Averaging five knots, the fleet raised the island of Dominica on November 3. Chanca noted that "The joy of the people was so great that it was wonderful to hear their cries and exclamations of pleasure; and they had good reason to be delighted, for they had become so wearied of bad living, and of working the water out of the ships, that all sighed most anxiously for land."

The confidence of Columbus during the passage was amazing. While other pilots had advised water rationing during the protracted cruise, the Admiral served it freely. On the night of November 2, when there was no reason apparent to others, he ordered all ships to take in sail and lie to. With his practiced eye Columbus had noted enough signs—changes in the color of the water and wind direction—to make him believe that land was near. When daylight revealed that his judg-

ment was correct, some of the men compared him to
Moses. As they closed Dominica they sighted several
other islands, and marveled at the mountainous beauty
before them. Unable to find a suitable anchorage at
Dominica, they moved to the leeward side of a neighboring island, which Columbus named Marie Galante,
and anchored there overnight. That evening, accompanied by a number of men, Columbus landed and took
possession of the islands.

They got under way from their roadstead anchorage
early on the morning of November 4 and steered for
a large island to the northwest. This the Admiral named
Santa Maria de Guadeloupe. At a distance of about 10
miles the men observed an immense waterfall that
"seemed to fall from the sky." A small caravel was
detached to reconnoiter the coast and search for an
anchorage. The captain of the caravel spotted a small
village, and went ashore to make contact with its inhabitants. The natives fled in haste at the sight of the
Spaniards, who looked about the village with great
curiosity. They noted cotton, parrots, and the usual
native huts, but recoiled in horror at the sight of four or
five bones of human arms and legs. The Indians had told
Columbus of the man-eating Caribs, and this was the
first of many evidences that they would find of this
loathsome custom. The stay at Guadelupe was extended
several days when one small expedition got lost in the
forest. Columbus sent out searching parties to no avail,
and was about to give them up when the emaciated
party returned after four frightening days in the forest.
In the meantime, other foraging expeditions had rounded
up quite a few natives, mostly women and boys, who
came with them voluntarily. These people were slaves

of the Caribs, taken prisoner from neighboring islands. From these unhappy people the Spaniards learned that the Caribs kept the young women as concubines, and would eat the children that they bore. Dr. Chanca described the Caribs' cannibalistic tendencies as follows:

> *"They say that man's flesh is so good, that there is nothing like it in the world; and this is pretty evident, for of the bones which we found in their houses, they had gnawed everything that could be gnawed . . . in one of the houses we found the neck of a man, undergoing the process of cooking in a pot. When they take boys as prisoners, they dismember them and make use of them until they grow up to manhood, and then when they wish to make a feast they kill and eat them, for they say that the flesh of boys and women is not good to eat."*

Taking the former slaves and a few Caribs with them, the ships got under way on November 10, and coasted northwest, discovering and naming the beautiful islands of the group: Montserrat, Antigua, Nevis, St. Kitts, St. Eustatius, Saba Islands, and St. Croix (their current names). At the St. Croix anchorage several Carib natives were cut off from shore by ships' boats. They put up a manful fight. Even the women in the canoe used a bow and arrow with good effect. In succession they cruised by St. John, St. Thomas, and Vieques to the south coast of Puerto Rico. On November 22 they anchored in Boquerón Bay. After an overnight rest they sailed northwest, making a landfall on the eastern tip of Hispaniola. Continuing westward they began to sight familiar landmarks, and Columbus hastened on to find his settlement at Navidad.

He put in at Monte Cristi for two days to search for a better settlement site than Navidad, and there found first signs that all was not well. Two bodies bound with rope were discovered near the river. On the next day they found two more. One was undoubtedly the corpse of a European because he had a heavy beard. Sensing impending disaster, Columbus made for Navidad and arrived offshore on the 27th. He fired guns to announce his arrival, but there was no answering signal. A canoe with several natives came out to the anchored fleet, and asked to see "the Admiral." The leader was a cousin of Guacanagari, and he bore ill tidings. He did not tell the whole truth—that the garrison had been wiped out—but he did say that many had died. Later investigation showed that the Spanish colonists had slowly gotten out of hand. Diego de Harana could not restrain some of the wilder men who quarreled over women and treasure. They made foraging raids for both in the interior and aroused the wrath of a native cacique, who decided to attack Navidad in force. Although Guacanagari and a few men tried to help, the colonists were killed.

The fate of his first colony saddened Columbus, but he determined to build another settlement nevertheless. After a few days' barter in which he obtained a respectable amount of gold, he decided to beat eastward in search of a better site for his next settlement. Moreover, according to Dr. Chanca, he "had tidings of gold in that direction." The tedious passage against the easterly trades exhausted his men, and his domestic animals began to perish from hardship. In desperation, on January 2 he gave up his battle with the trade winds and put into a sheltered harbor. Here he decided to found his new city, named Isabella in honor of his queen.

Dr. Chanca was overly optimistic about the location. He noted that the land was "very rich for all purposes" and that the waters teemed with fish that were "more wholesome than those of Spain." The men promptly planted vegetables, laid out streets, and began erecting shelters. Columbus sent two parties of men inland in search of gold. He was aware that he had to send some of his ships back to Spain for more supplies, and reasoned that his requests would be better received if they carried some treasure to his rulers. After a search of about three weeks the men returned with glorious tales of gold abounding along riverbanks, and brought in a reasonable number of nuggets. There was great rejoicing, despite the plague of sickness that had swept the camp. Dr. Chanca concluded his letter with the optimistic theme that their highnesses "may henceforth regard themselves as the most prosperous and wealthy Sovereigns in the world . . . on the return of the ships from their next voyage, they will be able to carry back such a quantity of gold as will fill with amazement all who hear of it."

The damp hot climate and hordes of mosquitoes soon brought malaria, and in a few weeks there was hardly a healthy man in the city. Columbus himself fell ill, but he gathered enough strength to write his sovereigns a report. In this memorandum of January 30, 1494, he recounted his discoveries and told of the fate of Navidad. He went into great detail about the kind of supplies that he needed, and suggested that Spain engage in slave trade as a way to underwrite the costs. (The

This *sculptured portrait of Christopher Columbus was saved from the
wreck of the Spanish battleship* Cristóbal Colón *during the Spanish-
American War. It now stands in Mahan Hall at the U.S. Naval Academy.*

The Jovius portrait of Christopher Columbus.

A representation of Columbus at work on his map making.

An idealized portrait of Columbus from a Venetian mosaic.

Another imaginary representation of Columbus (Metropolitan Museum of Art). No portrait of him was ever painted during his lifetime.

Representation of Columbus' 1492 fleet of caravels. Santa Maria *is in foreground.* Niña *and* Pinta *in background are shown here with lateen sails, but were actually square-rigged.*

A fanciful engraving of Columbus at the court of Queen Isabella.

A representation of Columbus before the Council of Salamanca.

Two interpretations of Columbus' embarkation from Palos in Spain on his historic first voyage.

A scene depicted in dozens of representations, this is a German artist's interpretation of the famous landing at San Salvador on October 12, 1492. Note initials of Ferdinand and Isabella on Columbus' standards, claiming the newly discovered lands for Spain.

An artist's interpretation of the caravel Santa Maria *being pounded to pieces on the coast of Hispaniola.*

A sketch by Columbus.

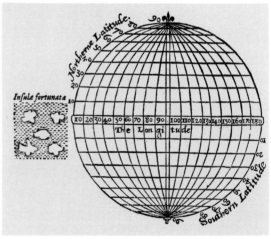

This sketch after Blundevile shows how early longitude was reckoned from the Canary Islands (Insulae fortunatae). *In Columbus' time the Canaries were considered to be the most westerly land in the world. The discoveries made by Columbus caused a shift of the prime meridian 100 leagues westward by papal decree. (Courtesy, Bundy Library)*

monarchs generally agreed with all of his report, but they wisely suspended judgment on importation of slaves.) Entrusting his letter to Antonio de Torres, Columbus put him in command of twelve ships and saw them off to Spain. Although there is no record, he undoubtedly must have advised Antonio of the way to make passage home. The route that he took during his first return voyage soon became standard—northwest past the easterlies and home on the westerlies.

Columbus the administrator and island governor was not the spectacular success that Columbus the mariner was. Shortly after the ships had left, he discovered an incipient mutiny of discontents led by Bernal Diaz. He punished the lesser leaders and sent Diaz back to Spain for trial. As a precaution, he gathered most of the colonists' weapons and placed them aboard a ship which was commanded by a man whom he trusted.

Impatient with the inactivity of Isabella and "city" life, Columbus decided to go into the hills himself in search of gold. He put his weak, mild brother Diego in command of Isabella, got a force of about 400 men together, and marched inland. On the slope of the Cibao Mountains he found a rich plain with a clear river, and erected a fort as a way station between Isabella and the gold mines that he hoped to dig. Everywhere he went he heard tales of great caches of gold "over there" or "over that mountain." Unfortunately, he never found that mysterious mine.

Returning to Isabella at the end of March he found more sickness, and worst of all, the prospects of a famine. Columbus was used to having all hands on deck in times of emergency at sea. Accordingly, he saw nothing wrong in making all hands—the proud Castilian nobles and priests included—turn to menial labor to get supplies in. This high-handed disregard for breeding aroused more antagonism against the "foreign" leader of the expedition.

Wisely Columbus hit upon a scheme to ease the tension. He put his favorite cavalier, Alonso de Hojeda, in charge of 250 men and sent them to his inland fort. They were to make their headquarters there, and scour the country in search of more gold. This was a mission that pleased the hot-tempered Castilians, who were more than willing to leave the hot lowlands of Isabella for the relatively cool mountains. Moreover, this quest promised action and adventure, which was much better than common labor.

The urge for adventure caught Columbus' fancy. He was tired of the cares of an administrator and longed for the feel of a deck beneath his feet and a cool breeze at sea. His search for Cipangu still beckoned him beyond the horizon, where Cuba (and the golden cities of Cathay and Cipangu) lay. Taking three small caravels which were suitable for shallow-water exploration, the Admiral put his brother Diego in command ashore and eagerly sailed west with a fair breeze.

CHAPTER 9

SEARCH FOR
THE KHAN

AS Columbus had demonstrated in his successful first voyage, whenever he had a conviction about something he could not be easily dissuaded from it. That same determination had once proven him right and the rest of the world wrong. Now, as he set out on his second exploratory sweep around Cuba, he had another opportunity to prove his original theory—that this land was a part of the Asian continent. Moreover, he intended to find the Grand Khan and the cities whose golden roofs glistened in the sun. In this way he would prove conclusively that the many islands that he had discovered lay off the coast of Asia, and that the Orient with its riches was just over the horizon to the west.

They weighed anchor at Isabella on April 24 and dropped in at the former site of Navidad. Columbus wanted to confer with Guacanagari, who was still regarded with suspicion by most Spaniards. The cacique avoided him, but sent word that he would appear soon. Refusing to idle away more hours in this unprofitable pursuit, Columbus continued westward along the Haitian coast and across the Windward Passage in sultry weather. Reaching Cape Maisi, the eastern tip of Cuba, on April 29, the Admiral landed and claimed the territory for Spain with his usual colorful ceremony. The next day the three ships entered a wide bay, whose entrance was only "150 paces in width." This sheltered harbor was so large that Columbus named it Puerto Grande, but it is now known by its previous Indian name of Guantanamo. In later years these spacious waters have housed the entire United States fleet, which has used Guantanamo as a training base since the turn of the twentieth century.

The Spaniards found only a few cane huts and an Indian fishing party on the shore. The huts were empty, but there was a great quantity of fish about, some hanging from trees, and others roasting over live fires. The natives had fled, leaving this tempting meal for the hungry invaders. They polished off the fish in short order, but recoiled in disgust at roast iguana, which the Indians considered a delicacy. Through the efforts of their native interpreter, the Spaniards made contact with the fishermen, who, they learned, were on a mission to get quantities of fish for a banquet that their cacique was preparing. Columbus paid for the poached meal with a few trinkets and questioned the Indians about gold. They pointed to the south, where, they said, there was an island with large quantites of yellow metal. This aroused the expedition's curiosity, because it conformed to other leads given by inhabitants of the north coast of Cuba. Perhaps this was Babeque, the fabulous but elusive island of gold.

The thought so intrigued Columbus that he broke off

his coastal cruise two days later at Cape Cruz and steered south. Two days' southing brought a landfall on the beautiful island of Jamaica. On May 5 they put in to St. Ann's Bay, against the wishes and warlike gestures of the natives, who were not the least awed by the "great ships." Here the explorers were disappointed to find that none of the natives, whom they eventually pacified, wore ornaments of gold. Subsequent landings at Puerto Bueno and at Montego Bay confirmed their suspicion—this gold hunt was just another false trail.

Taking some time for repairs and calking, Columbus put parties ashore to gather wood and water. At Puerto Bueno the Spaniards had to handle hostile natives roughly before they reached an understanding. In a minor engagement, one cavalier loosed his dog on the Indians with great effect. This experiment proved so successful that it later became standard Spanish doctrine for Indian fighting. To the astonished natives, whose small dogs could not bark and were treated as domestic animals, a ferocious European hunting dog was a frightening thing. The Spaniards soon came to consider a dog to be "worth ten men against Indians."

Resolving to return to Jamaica for a more thorough exploration at a later date, Columbus left on May 13 and steered a course for Cape Cruz to the north. There he resumed his exploratory probe of Cuba's south coast, unknowingly committing his ships to some of the most dangerous shoal water sailing ever recorded. If Columbus, the blue-water sailor, had foreseen the ordeal that lay ahead in the tortuous channels, hidden reefs, and mudbanks, perhaps he would have picked a course well to the south of Cuba. However, history quickly forgets "discoverers" who keep clear of coastal waters and refuse to take chances. In this westing along the south coast of Cuba, Columbus firmly established himself as one of the greatest offshore seamen of all time. Perhaps his son Ferdinand's title of Chapter 57 of his biography of his father provides the best thumbnail description of this arduous voyage. It reads: "How the Admiral Endured Great Hardships and Toil as He Sailed Among Islands Innumerable." The chapter states that "By this time the Admiral was quite worn out, both on account of poor diet and because (aside from eight days when he was seriously indisposed) he had not undressed and slept a full night in bed from the time he left Spain until May 19th."

It might be added that Columbus found very little surcease from his constant vigil after May 19 and indeed until the end of this voyage. One thing is clear—Columbus was a good captain who felt his responsibility keenly and took a sailor's pride in professional accomplishment. In a revealing journal entry during the month of July he wrote:

"I am on the same ration as the others. May it please God that this be for His service and that of Your Highnesses. Were it only for myself, I would no longer bear such pains and dangers, for not a day passes that we do not look death in the face."

After a session like this, it is little wonder that he suffered a nervous collapse after his small fleet safely reached the familiar northern shores of Hispaniola in September.

The "innumerable islands" that they encountered in May received the romantic name of "Jardin de la

Reina" (the Queen's Garden). Columbus chose this collective name because it would have been almost impossible to give each islet a name. This group nestles just west of the Gulf of Guacanayabo, and even today is such a navigational challenge that few strangers to these waters will attempt to sail them. From May 14 to May 25 Columbus explored the coastal waters of Guacanayabo and threaded the tortuous channels of the Queen's Garden. On one day alone, he counted one hundred and sixty separate islands. The scenery was beautiful, and the men enjoyed the strange sights and fragrant air.

They came upon some Indian fishermen in the Garden who were quite unperturbed by the ship's sudden appearance. They were too busy fishing. Ingeniously these men used a pilot fish with a small retrieving line tied to its tail. This parasite would swim after its prey, and would fasten itself to a vulnerable spot on the target— usually the neck of a sea turtle or a larger fish. Then it would hang on tenaciously while the fisherman reeled in both the hunter and hunted. The Indians treated their pilot fish with great tenderness, stroking them and praising them after each catch.

Ferdinand, who accompanied Columbus on the fourth voyage, cruised through these same waters in 1503. So when he writes of the wonders and trials of this part of the second voyage, he writes from firsthand knowledge. For example, he described the daily afternoon thunderstorms, which caused Columbus great difficulty in the narrow channels, as follows:

"The sight of these islands or shoals all about them was frightening enough, but what was worse

was that each afternoon a dense mist rose over them in the eastern sky, with such thunder and lightning that it seemed a deluge was about to fall; when the moon came out it all vanished, dissolving part into rain and part into wind. This is such a common phenomenon that it happened each afternoon on that voyage; and I myself observed it when cruising among those islands in 1503."

On May 26 Columbus entered a bay that some thought might be an important channel. Fifteen miles inland they found that it was entirely landlocked, and that clear cool springwater poured into the sea at its northern shore. While Columbus did not name this area, it later received the name "Bahia de Cochinos," or Bay of Pigs—the scene of the disastrous Cuban rebel landing in 1962.

After a short rest, they continued west with movements that are difficult to trace. The reason is clear in Ferdinand's book: "This navigation in a maze of shoals and islands caused the Admiral much toil, for he had to steer now west, now north, now south, according to the disposition of the channels. And for all his care in making soundings and keeping lookouts in the roundtop, the ship often scraped bottom, there being innumerable shoals all about." Frequently he would send his smallest ship ahead, with the others following in her wake. On several occasions the *Niña* had to be kedged over a sandbar, a laborious process which opened her seams and let water into her stores of provisions. At length, the hard labor and poor diet began to tell on the crews, and they approached Columbus about turning back. When he was a scant fifty miles from the western tip of Cuba, he finally acquiesced, but not without exacting a peculiar oath from his men.

Historians have written realms of speculation about his "exploration by certification." On June 12 he caused all men to swear before the staff notary that Cuba was a part of the Asian mainland. To show that he meant business, he added a provision for punishment of any signatory who later changed his mind. The rule was quite clear: an officer would be fined 10,000 maravedis; a sailor would have his tongue cut out and receive 100 lashes.

Having completed his exploration by affidavit, he turned back, and promptly wasted ten days in a vain effort to get clear to the southeast. He searched for a passage near the Isle of Pines until the difficulties of breaking clear persuaded him to retrace his former track to Cape Cruz. The difficulties of his long beat to windward are hard to imagine. But Columbus, always the optimist and a cheerful leader, reminded his men that the return trip would be easier—for they had eaten almost all of their provisions and consequently drew less water! Not a word was said about short rations, the incessant vigil, the evening thunderstorms, manning the pumps and groundings.

While the voyage yielded no treasures, it gave the men enough material to spin yarns for the rest of their days. They saw herds of turtles that covered the surface of the sea. Clouds of crows and pigeons frequently shut out the sun. Occasionally swarms of butterflies would be borne out to sea on a land breeze, and would dance around the rigging in a confusion of color until the evening storm blew them away. The men picked large conch shells from the sandy bottom, and shucked bushels of oysters in a vain search for pearls. They passed through seas white as milk, where the turbulence of the waves kept a limestone bottom in suspension with the water. And as often, too, they would encounter water black as ink, followed soon after by a bright emerald green. In retrospect years later, when memories of aching backs, tired muscles, and little sleep had drifted into the background, these strange and beautiful sights stood out clearly in their minds' eyes.

The vagaries of the sea were brought home to them with sudden impact. On July 17, as they worked their way across the open sea between the Queen's Garden and Cape Cruz, a violent storm almost capsized the ships. *Niña* rolled over until water poured in on the main deck—she escaped foundering by miraculous luck and some furious pumping by her exhausted crew. July 18 found them at Cape Cruz, where they had started two long months before. Here they rested and waited for a favorable wind, enjoying the friendliness of the Indians, who received them eagerly and vied with one another in offering fruit, food, fresh water, and good will.

On the 22nd the tired ships ventured into Windward Passage and steered south for Jamaica, which Columbus had promised himself he would visit again and explore. He returned to Montego Bay and then sailed around Jamaica's western tip to completely circumnavigate the island. Compared to the swampy mangrove coasts of southern Cuba, this was a pleasure cruise. Ferdinand notes that the land was "so green and smiling, abounding in food and densely populated" that Columbus "thought it unsurpassed by none."

The Admiral was particularly fond of a roadstead

that he named Bahia de las Vacas (now called Portland Bight). As he weighed anchor to leave this "Bay of Cows," he was visited by a native chief, who came with his wife, two sons, and two daughters. The cacique offered to join the expedition with all of his family, in order to visit Spain and pay homage to the King and Queen. Columbus agreed to accept them as royal subjects, but refused to take them with him on the grounds that he had many places to visit and poor accommodations for a family of high position.

Columbus took departure from Jamaica on August 19 and crossed to Cape Tiburon, the southwestern tip of Hispaniola. Somehow his sense of dead reckoning must have failed him, for he did not realize that he had returned to Hispaniola until a local Indian addressed him as "Almirante." He could have returned to Isabella more quickly via the coast on Windward Passage, but he chose to continue eastward in order to circumnavigate the large island. Putting a few men ashore with instructions to cross overland to Isabella and inform Diego Columbus of his whereabouts, Columbus pushed stubbornly on. Near the eastern tip at Mona Passage, he named a small island La Bella Saonese in honor of the Italian town of Savona. With his seaman's sense for bad weather, Columbus predicted the arrival of a tropical storm and took shelter on the leeward side of the island. Ferdinand noted that a full eclipse of the moon occurred while the storm blew out, and concluded that the eclipse had prolonged the bad weather.

After a five-day wait, the Admiral got under way and sailed around Cape Engano for a downwind leg back to Isabella. At this point he fell ill. Ferdinand called the illness a fever; other biographers suggest a nervous breakdown. Columbus fell into a coma, and "lost his sight, memory, and all his other senses." The ship's officers hastened back to Isabella, arriving on September 29, and tenderly put the Admiral ashore. When he awoke some time later, Christopher Columbus was pleased to see his brother Bartholomew standing by his bed. Here was another man that he could trust and confide in. Eagerly the two brothers brought each other up to date, and filled in the blanks caused by years of separation.

CHAPTER 10

SPANISH STEEL

THE next year and a half of Columbus' life, from September, 1494, to March, 1496, is a period that his admirers would like to forget. While he was not guilty personally, his poor administration was responsible for unusually cruel and harsh treatment of the Tainos Indians of Hispaniola.

During his absence, the party of men that he had dispatched to the interior under command of Pedro Margarit had almost gone berserk. Instead of policing the province of Cibao, they roamed the more fertile foothills, demanding food, gold, and women from the natives. As these excesses continued, the men grew more vicious, and were soon given to torture, rape, and murder. Eventually the Indians fought back, falling upon small bands of isolated Spaniards and killing them to a man. Margarit and his religious cohort, Fray Buil, treated Diego Columbus with haughty disdain and refused to pay any attention to his repeated protests. When, after several months, they realized that they had no future in Hispaniola and that there was little gold to be had, they feared retaliation for their insubordination. Rather than face the Admiral, they seized three of Bartholomew Columbus' ships in the harbor and returned to Spain. There they spread damaging stories about the rule of the Columbus brothers, and mended their own fences in court to defend their past misconduct.

When Columbus returned from his exploratory sweep of Cuba, Jamaica, and Hispaniola, he was in no condition to look after island administration. By title and official edict he was Viceroy and Governor, and the supreme representative of the crown in the Indies. In view of his own infirmities, he appointed his brother Bartholomew second in command with the title of Adelantado, or "deputy." Ineffectual Diego Columbus, who was very devout and longed to become a priest, willingly turned over his administrative responsibilities to his brother. Bartholomew was a capable man, an excellent seaman, and a fair but tough administrator. Yet he lacked the intellectual depth of Christopher, as well as that "something extra"—the spark that made the latter a genius instead of a run-of-the-mill ship captain. Nevertheless, Bartholomew was a steadying influence and was fiercely loyal to his more talented brother.

Even a casual observer would recognize, from all contemporary accounts of the explorations of Columbus, that he was a patient and understanding man. His early relations with the natives of "the Indies" give ample proof of his forbearance. Whenever he returned to an island or a port for the second time, he was welcomed by the local inhabitants, who brought presents, fresh water, and food. The fierce Caribs were the only exception. Still, even against these determined antagonists, Columbus was reluctant to use the superior weapons of his own civilization. His usual practice was to fire harmlessly into the air, trying to win his point by example and not by terror. Yet the situation in Hispaniola in 1494 was entirely different. The small Spanish colony was nestled in a corner of a large territory, surrounded by 300,000 natives whose temper and disposition grew more menacing each day. Already they had tasted blood. First, Caonabo had wiped out the garrison at Navidad in 1493. Now another cacique, Guatiguana, had killed a scouting party of ten Spaniards, and had set fire to a hut that housed forty sick men from Isabella. Not a one escaped. If Guatiguana could have united the Indians of other tribes and provinces there is little doubt that he could have driven the Spaniards into the sea.

As soon as he was well enough, Columbus decided that it was a time for action, not words. This situation called for Spanish steel, or the whole colony would suffer the consequences. Accordingly, from his sickbed he directed Bartholomew to send a punitive force into Guatiguana's province. With the fierceness and cruelty that characterized the Spanish explorers of the fifteenth and sixteenth centuries, the armed men hunted down their hapless opponents. They killed hundreds and took as many prisoners. The hardiest of these were packed off to Spain in February, 1495, for the slave markets of Europe. In the darkskinned natives of Hispaniola, Columbus had found a substitute for gold—at least he thought he had. But this unfortunate venture failed. Many prisoners died of exposure during the return trip, and the others languished away in the "cold" climate of Spain. It was an unprofitable venture from the beginning, and it was practiced without royal sanction and against the open disapproval of Queen Isabella. It is difficult for some to believe that Columbus, who

97

watched over his men at sea like a mother hen, and who would wait days for a lost foraging party, could condone slavery. Yet it is evident from his journal of the first voyage that one of his first thoughts about the natives of San Salvador was that they were docile and would make good slaves.

Brother Diego Columbus also sailed with the ships of Antonio de Torres in February. King Ferdinand had written to Columbus for assistance in determining a new line of demarcation. He had asked for the explorer's presence in court, but permitted him the alternative of sending one of his brothers instead. While the offer was tempting and there were many other good reasons for Columbus' presence in court, he was unwilling to leave before he had put down the Indian rebellion. So Diego, loaded with maps, journals, and instructions from Columbus, was returned to Spain with a twofold mission. He planned to assist in the demarcation conferences and also to protect the Admiral's interests back home.

At this point, the tolerance that Columbus had shown cacique Guacanagari was repaid in full. The local chieftain visited Isabella and informed the Admiral of plans for a combined Indian attack on the settlement. The other primary caciques, Guatiguana, Caonabo, and Behechio, had begun to realize the folly of their previous isolation. Deciding to move quickly before the Indian plans turned into action, Columbus marched into Guatiguana's province with a force of infantry and cavalry and a pack of fierce dogs. Although the Spaniards were outnumbered one hundred to one, they routed the Indian horde in a terrible massacre. According to one chronicler, "the woods were filled with flying and shrieking savages" who were hunted down by horsemen and bloodhounds. Once the battle was over, Columbus gathered in another large group of prisoners for the next slave ship returning to Spain.

Of all the Indian leaders, Caonabo was the most cunning and warlike. His successes against the invaders were legend. Columbus realized that he had to eliminate Caonabo in order to restore peace, but the chieftain's mountain stronghold was more formidable than the rest. His problem was solved by Captain Hojeda, the dashing hidalgo who excelled in the arts of war and feats of strength. Taking 10 of his best horsemen, Hojeda boldly went into Caonabo's village for a parley. There he threw himself on the chivalry and hospitality of the cacique, who admired bravery in friend or foe. Caonabo received him courteously and soon agreed to go with him to Isabella for a peace conference with Columbus. Taking a strong bodyguard he set out with Hojeda's cavalry. Along the way he was tricked into mounting behind Hojeda's saddle and fastening himself securely with a pair of handcuffs which the Spanish captain assured him were valuable ornaments usually worn by visiting dignitaries. At that Hojeda and his men broke out from the native bodyguard and galloped back to Isabella with their prisoner. Rather than try Caonabo at Isabella, Columbus decided to return the furious cacique to Spain. Here the story of Caonabo runs out; he remained a prisoner until he died at sea en route to Seville for his trial.

With his primary foe safely out of the way, Columbus undertook a methodical campaign to put down all opposition. Spanish steel, Spanish horses, and footmen with their bloodhounds routed every force that tried to oppose them. As Ferdinand wrote, Columbus "re-duced the Indians to such obedience and tranquillity" that they willingly worked as plantation slaves and paid a tribute in gold. In Cibao every person above the age of fourteen was required to produce a hawk's bell full of gold dust every three months. Others had to pay twenty-five pounds of cotton.

Columbus did not realize that the gold ornaments that the Indians wore when he first arrived represented years of family industry. His demands were impossible. At length the despondent Indians took to the forests and mountain slopes where many died of starvation or else killed themselves with the poison of the cassava root. The invaders never let up, and hunted them out like wild game to return them for punishment and more hard labor. These measures made the island so peaceful, said Ferdinand, that "a Christian could safely go wherever he pleased, and the Indians themselves offered to carry him pickaback."

In October, 1495, Juan Aguado, the sovereigns' "groom from the chambers," arrived at Isabella with authority to investigate the complaints and discontent of the settlers. Columbus bowed to his superior author-ity, effectively permitting his own replacement as vice-roy. Aguado listened to complaints, took depositions, and soon drew up a list of accusations to send back to Spain. Realizing that his situation was fast becoming perilous, the Admiral decided to return home himself in March, 1496.

With the faithful *Niña* and one other caravel, *India*, Columbus set out for Spain. This time he tried a different route, retracing his earlier steps to Marie Galante. Against the easterly trades this leg of the voyage was painfully slow, requiring thirty days. Alarmed that his supply of food would not last the rest of the crossing, he put in at Guadeloupe to replenish. In this land of the Caribs the Spaniards met temporary opposition—again finding that Carib women were good fighters. The ships remained at Guadeloupe a fortnight while the crew prepared a stock of cassava bread and filled the water kegs.

All was ready by April 20, when the crowded ships set out for a monotonous seven weeks' voyage across the Atlantic. Near the end of it, all hands were down to a daily ration of six ounces of bread and a pint and a half of water. Ferdinand said that some of the crew proposed to eat the Indians that they carried. Others thought it would be better to save food by heaving the miserable prisoners overboard, "and would have done it, too, if the Admiral had not forbidden it." The next day, June 8, when the accompanying pilots "went about like men who were lost or blind," Columbus made a landfall on the coast of Portugal between Lisbon and Cape St. Vincent. "From that time on," bragged Ferdinand, "the seamen regarded the Admiral as most expert and admirable in matters of navigation." Three days later they anchored in Cádiz, as wretched a group as ever made a long voyage and lived to tell about it.

PART IV

Third Voyage

CHAPTER 11

BECALMED
IN SPAIN

COLUMBUS went ashore at Cádiz wearing the rough cloth robe of a Franciscan monk. Always a devout man, he turned to religion more and more as he advanced in age. However, many a sailor has prayed for a safe return to port, and has vowed to perform some religious duty in return. After his first voyage Columbus made pilgrimages of thanksgiving for surviving the winter storms. It is quite likely that he made a few personal vows on the second trip, when starvation followed in the wake of his ship.

Pausing long enough to dispatch a letter to Bartholomew with the captain of a caravel sailing for Hispaniola, Columbus took lodgings in Seville with Andres Bernaldez, the curate of Las Palacios. In the peace and quiet of the Bernaldez home he regained his health. After about a month he received a courteous letter from the sovereigns, inviting him to come to court and discuss his most recent adventures; nothing was said about the many complaints and accusations of his colonists. Leading a cavalcade of Indians, he marched through the country toward Burgos, being careful to have the chieftains wear golden ornaments whenever the parade entered a town or city.

His reception in court was gracious, but somewhat cooler than before. The sovereigns listened attentively and promised to provide ships for a third voyage. However, they were busy with affairs of state and plans for the marriage of the crown prince, Don Juan, to Princess Margarita of Austria. Moreover, there was difficulty with France, which at the time threatened minor hostilities and was a potential drain on the royal treasury. These pressing matters pushed exploration into the background, and Columbus had to wait almost two years before he could equip another fleet. It was not a pleasant stay, for as Columbus said in his history of the third voyage, "I had hoped, when I left the Indies, to find repose in Spain; whereas on the contrary, I experienced nothing but opposition and vexation."

He was referring to the general attitude of people about his discoveries. By then enough adventurers had returned from Hispaniola to spread knowledge of the heat, mosquitoes, and fever that plagued Europeans in that tropic land. Moreover, no one believed that there was much gold or any other form of wealth on the island. The excitement and anticipation which marked the preparations for his second voyage now turned to reluctance and scorn. Too many Spaniards rested in the graveyards of Hispaniola, and there had been very little to show for their sacrifices.

Despite this attitude, Columbus went steadfastly on his way, planning his next trip, scheming with his friends in court, and looking after his personal affairs. Queen Isabella saw to it that his rights as delineated in the patent of the first voyage were reaffirmed. He retained his title, his coat of arms, and his right to a portion of the revenues from the islands.

As a rather desperate means to replenish their treasury, the sovereigns had, in 1495, granted seagoing Spaniards the privilege of making exploratory voyages at their own expense. This business proposition highly favored the crown, which took a major share of all profits yet bore no part of any losses. Columbus protested that this edict undermined his own rights, and finally persuaded the sovereigns to amend the original order with the statement that they did not intend "in any way to affect the rights of Don Christopher Columbus." This amendment appeared in June, 1497, but only after several expeditions had sailed.

In the summer of 1497 Columbus received royal instructions for the third voyage, as well as a modest credit in the treasury to finance the venture. Anticipating difficulty in obtaining colonists, the crown offered full pardon to criminals who would go and spend time in Hispaniola. The length of stay was determined from a sliding scale which was related to the nature of the crime for which they were imprisoned. This was the first such offer in connection with the New World, but history shows that most other nations engaged in founding colonies abroad had to resort to a similar expedient. Good examples of these are the penal colony of Georgia in North America and the early settlements in Australia.

From all accounts it appears that Columbus still enjoyed good relations with his sovereigns, but the seeds of discontent were widely scattered among powerful members of the court. Ferdinand, who had spent most of his young life in the court as a page, puts it this way: ". . . later, because of lying reports of spiteful and

envious men, they changed their demeanor and permitted injuries and offenses to be done to him." He
mentions the "mortal hatred" of Juan de Fonseca as
follows: "At Seville, whither the Admiral departed
from the court, the despatch of the fleet was much
delayed through neglect and mismanagement on the
part of the royal officials, and especially of Don Juan
de Fonseca, Archdean of Seville and later Bishop of
Burgos." Ferdinand does not mention that one of Fonseca's employees was so insolent to Columbus that the
Admiral knocked him down and physically kicked him
off his flagship. This display of temper was magnified
by Fonseca to such an extent that it played an important part in the change of the crown's attitude toward
Columbus.

Having obtained royal permission to entail his estate,
Columbus made out a *mayorazzo*, or will, in February,
1498. This was mentioned in the first chapter of this
book as an important document that pinpoints the
Admiral's birthplace as having been Genoa. The will
provided for the succession of his heirs, who would
inherit his wealth and title. Among other requirements
he insisted on the creation of a fund in the Bank of St.
George in Genoa for the purpose of financing an expedition to recover the Holy Sepulcher when feasible.

Putting young Diego and Ferdinand in court as pages
to Queen Isabella (Prince Juan died five months after
his marriage) Columbus now had his personal affairs
well in hand. He turned his full energy toward preparing his ships for sea. In late May, 1498, his six caravels
dropped downriver from Seville to the little seaport
of San Lucar, where the Admiral went on board and
prepared to sail.

CHAPTER 12

THE GULF
OF PEARLS

THE third voyage is best described by Columbus himself. In a lengthy letter to his sovereigns, dated October, 1498, he gives one of the most straightforward accounts of any of his great voyages. It is characteristic of the man that he did not emphasize the superb seamanship that was necessary to explore these strange coasts and to bring his ships safely to Hispaniola. As usual he took that for granted, and once again treated a tremendous accomplishment of dead-reckoning sailing as a routine, everyday matter.

Leaving San Lucar on May 30, with "six vessels loaded with provisions and other things to relieve settlers on Hispaniola," the Admiral sailed for the Madeira Islands. Perhaps for sentimental reasons he stopped at Porto Santo where he had honeymooned with his young wife, Felipa, in 1479. From Madeira he took the familiar leg to Gomera in the Canary Islands. Having made plans to explore south of Hispaniola, he divided his fleet and sent three relief ships directly to his brother Bartholomew at Santo Domingo. (During Columbus' two-year wait in Spain, Bartholomew, according to plan, had begun to move the settlement of Isabella to a new location—Santo Domingo.) He gave the relief expedition explicit sailing directions, which they managed to botch—instead of beating the Admiral to Santo Domingo, as they would have done with a direct route, they arrived after he did.

The fleet parted company off the island of Ferro, where Columbus took his flagship and two smaller caravels on a southerly heading for Boa Vista in the Cape Verde Islands. He had difficulty obtaining fresh provisions there, and was disenchanted with the islands, which, he said, were named incorrectly, "for they are so barren that nothing green was to be seen there, and the people so sickly that I did not venture to remain among them." At the time of his visit to Boa Vista, it was a haven for lepers who would come from Europe to be cured. They attributed their recovery to a diet of turtle meat and the medicinal properties of turtle blood, which they smeared over their sores. No wonder Columbus did not wish to tarry there.

On leaving Boa Vista he steered southwest, intending to reach the latitude of Sierra Leone before going due west. Unwittingly he headed right into the doldrums, that dreaded belt of calms just above the equator where many a sailing ship has come to grief. Columbus thought the intensity of the heat was such that "both ships and men would have been burnt up, and everything got into such a state of confusion, that no man dared go below deck to attend to the securing of the water cask and provisions." There was not a breath of air nor a ripple on the water, but the equatorial current gradually carried his ships clear. On July 22, "it pleased the Lord" to send Columbus a favorable east wind, which raised everyone's spirits and cooled off the ships. He headed due west, abandoning his plan to touch the Equator. Columbus had had his fill of equatorial calms and now realized that his freshwater supplies were running out. The ships made excellent time for the next nine days. On July 31 the food and water situation was so desperate that Columbus gave up his westerly heading and changed course to the northwest toward Hispaniola. Shortly afterward, Alonzo Perez, from the fishing village of Huelva, spotted land on the port bow. As they drew closer, Columbus could make out three peaks, so he named the island Trinidad in honor of the Trinity. His actual landfall was at Cape Galeota, the southeastern tip of the island. Once more Columbus had before him the sailor's delight of coasting strange shores and making discoveries. With eager anticipation he approached land, noting that it "was very beautiful, and as fresh and green as the gardens of Valencia in the month of March."

The island of Trinidad lies just off the coast of Venezuela, and forms the eastern boundary of the Gulf of Paria. Two fingers of Trinidad, one at its northern extremity and one at its southern end, pointed westward toward the continent of South America. At the tip of each finger there is a small opening of water that separates Trinidad from the mainland. Through these openings, or channels, the waters of the Gulf of Paria run at the speed of a millrace. They are hastened on their way by the equatorial current, which strikes the coast at this point, and the great South American watershed that pours into the sea from the estuaries of the Orinoco River near the southern entrance to the gulf.

Columbus sailed west from Cape Galeota toward the southern entrance of the Gulf of Paria (which he named

Golfo de la Ballena) looking for a watering place. On August 1 he saw land to the south, and assumed that it was another island. Although he did not know it, he was looking at the coast of South America, probably the first time that any European had done so. At Punta de la Plaza (now called Erin Point) he anchored in a small bay and sent watering parties ashore. Ferdinand recalls that "the sailors went ashore with much merriment and took water from a pleasant brook." After their previous stretch in the humid doldrums, and several weeks at sea on water rations, the men had a field day and drank their fill.

Everywhere there were signs of life, but the natives remained out of sight. On August 2 the ships continued west along the southern coast of Trinidad, riding with the strong current. They swung through the southern entrance to the Gulf of Paria at slack water and anchored near Sandy Point (Punta del Arenal). For two days they gathered wood and fresh water. The high point of this stay occurred on August 3, when a canoe full of native men came out to look the ships over. Columbus thought that the Indians were "well-proportioned, and not dark black, but whiter than any other Indians" that he had seen; also, he said they were "of very graceful gesture and handsome forms, wearing their hair long and straight. . . ." His usual tricks to entice the visitors alongside failed, so Columbus ordered some of his sailors to dance with the accompaniment of pipe and drum, hoping that this would whet their guests' curiosity. On the contrary, the natives must have interpreted these strange antics as a war dance, because they seized their bows and fired arrows at the ship. Columbus ordered his crossbowmen to return the fire. The canoe did an about-face as the Indians beat a hasty retreat toward the smaller caravels. There they were treated well, and soon struck up a trade, exchanging native goods for hawks' bells and other trifles. This was the Spaniards' only contact with natives on the island of Trinidad.

Columbus studied the currents of the southern gulf entrance, which he had named Serpent's Mouth (Boca de la Sierpe), and concluded that it would be impossible to make his way back through the same exit. The current was too swift. Reasoning that this rush of water demanded another outlet from the gulf, Columbus decided to sail north to see for himself. He had another reason for wanting to move. On the night of August 3, he saw a phenomenal wave bearing down on the ships. As the Admiral put it, "In the dead of night while I was on deck, I heard an awful roaring that came from the south toward the ship; I stopped to observe what it might be, and I saw the sea rolling from west to east like a mountain as high as a ship, and approaching by little and little; on top of this rolling sea came a mighty wave roaring with a frightful noise, and with all this terrific uproar were other conflicting currents, producing, as I have already said, a sound as of breakers upon the rocks. To this day [he wrote this two months later] I have a vivid recollection of the dread I then felt, lest the ship founder under the force of that tremendous sea; but it passed by. . . ." The wave actually passed under the ships, snapping the hawser of one of the caravels but otherwise doing no damage.

They sailed across the Gulf of Paria without incident, and on its northern side Columbus found the entrance that he had expected. This one was smaller than the Serpent's Mouth, and even more fear-inspiring. Water rushed through the passage with a tremendous roaring, leaving in its wake boiling eddies and frothing foam. Deciding not to risk a passage, Columbus crossed over to the South American coast and sailed west, inside the gulf, noting that the water became sweeter "and more wholesome" with each league made good. On August 5, he anchored and sent a party ashore. The men found fruit and monkeys, but no people.

Columbus moved farther west, at length anchoring in the mouth of a river, probably the Rio Guiria. Here he took possession of the land for the crown, and finally established contact with the natives. He was pleased to see some of them wearing gold and pearl ornaments. Upon inquiring where the gold came from, the natives pointed to the hills in the west. Pearls, they indicated, were west and also north, on another coastline. The Admiral did not investigate these vague directions, because his provisions were running low and he had to move on. Unable to locate a passage to the ocean in the western end of the gulf, he gave up and returned to the boisterous northern channel that he had named Dragon's Mouth (Boca del Dragon). Anchoring near the entrance, he studied the currents. The boiling eddies and whirlpools could be caused by rocks just below the surface. However, he reasoned that they were the result of fresh currents seeking the sea and salt water set in motion by the tide. If this were correct, he needed only a favorable wind to make his way through. Actually, he had little choice, for there was no other feasible way out.

During the early morning of August 13, Columbus got his small fleet under way and stood toward the pass, reluctantly departing the Gulf of Pearls (as he named the inner part of the Gulf of Paria). The wind failed as he was sailing through Boca del Dragon, and, according to Ferdinand, "he ran great danger of being dashed to pieces," but the current, which he feared most, carried him clear and into the open sea. Once in blue water again, he changed course to the west and traversed the true "Pearl Coast" without touching it.

Columbus was now a sick man. The gout that he had acquired from countless hours of exposure during previous voyages began to plague him in earnest. In addition, his eyes began to trouble him, probably from lack of sleep and inflammation caused by the sun's bright glare. He remembered his physical lapse at the end of the exploration of Cuba in 1494, and so gave up any ideas that he might have had to explore this coast on his port hand. This decision, as it turned out, cost him the opportunity of discovering the real pearl coast—an honor that fell to another Spanish adventurer, Hojeda, a short while later. He did, however, chance upon some pearl fishermen, who eagerly turned over "three pounds of pearls" for some bits of Spanish china. During this leg of his cruise, Columbus sighted the islands of Tobago and Grenada to the north of Trinidad, and concluded his westward sailing at the island of Margarita, just north of the "Cabode Conchas," Venezuela, which is probably the point now called Punta Escuda Blanca.

While the Admiral was under the weather with gout and inflamed eyes, his pilots maintained a course well clear of land, and let him rest. His body was fatigued, but his active mind grappled with all these recent discoveries. It was here, according to Ferdinand, that he concluded that the land bordering the Gulf of Pearls was not a series of islands, but a continent. His reasons were ". . . the great size of the Golfo de las Perlas and of the rivers issuing from it; because all the water in that sea was sweet; because Esdras in Chapter 8 of his fourth book says that of the seven parts of this sphere only one is covered with water; and also because all the Indians in the Cannibal Islands had told them that to the south there lay a very large continent."

If he had stopped there, perhaps there would have been less controversy over the "Discovery of America," and the naming of the continent. However, Columbus went on to reason that this continent was really the Garden of Eden, which rested on a swelling apex of the earth "like a woman's nipple." He connected everything that he had read of the superstition and fancy of the past to support his argument, and included it in his letter to the sovereigns. "There are great indications," he wrote, "of this being the terrestrial paradise, for its site coincides with the opinion of the holy and wise theologians whom I have mentioned; and moreover, other evidences agree with the supposition, for I have never either read or heard of fresh water coming in so large a quantity . . . and if the water of which I speak does not proceed from the earthly paradise, it appears to be still more marvelous, for I do not believe that there is any river in the world so large or so deep."

In that last phrase, Columbus had the truth at his fingertips. However, Americus Vespucius visited this area shortly afterward (there is some controversy as to the exact date) and submitted a much clearer and more objective report of what he had seen. As this was the first published account of the "New World," it was widely read and led to the belief that Americus Vespucius was its first discoverer. It was in this manner that the continents of North America and South America were named.

On August 15 Columbus called a halt to his explorations and headed north again for Hispaniola. Although he had not seen a familiar landmark since departing the Cape Verde Islands, he expected to hit his target—a point east of Santo Domingo—on the nose. To his great chagrin, however, he made one of the few errors of his long lifetime of dead reckoning, and on August 20 arrived at Alta Vela, an island off the southernmost tip of Hispaniola about 100 miles west of Santo Domingo. He attributed his error, quite correctly, to the set of a strong westerly current, but he was annoyed to have missed his landfall by such a wide margin.

So the ships anchored near Alta Vela and waited while Columbus searched for an Indian messenger to carry a letter to his brother at Santo Domingo. Having accomplished this, he weighed anchor and began the long beat to windward against the opposing current. As the fleet moved out of its anchorage, the lookouts spotted a caravel approaching from the east. It proved to be Bartholomew Columbus, the adelantado of Hispaniola, who had learned of this third voyage and was out at sea in search of his famous brother. Despite the grave news that he brought with him, the two brothers had a joyful reunion.

CHAPTER 13

SANTO DOMINGO

AS the ships slowly made their way toward Santo Domingo, Bartholomew Columbus brought Christopher up to date on the affairs of the island. During two and a half troubled years, the adelantado had been a vigorous, forceful ruler. But he had had to deal with the laziness of the workmen, open hostility of the Spaniards, and native conspiracies. According to his brother's instructions, he had founded a new settlement on the eastern end of the island, naming it New Isabella. This first permanent settlement in the New World soon acquired the name of Santo Domingo, as it is still called today.

Bartholomew had then established a chain of military posts between Isabella and Santo Domingo, and begun a gradual movement of men and supplies between the two settlements. Meanwhile, the few crops that had been planted had failed through neglect, and additional supplies were needed from Spain. With provisions running short and many of the people sick, the colonists' hope began to fade and many voiced their open discontent with the adelantado.

The typical Spanish adventurer in Hispaniola hated work, lived only to search for gold, and passed his idle hours in dissolution and intrigue. It was not difficult for a man like Roldan, the chief judge of the island, to take advantage of the growing dissatisfaction with the Columbus brothers and form a party of rebellion. Roldan also conspired with native chieftains, who were tired of paying tribute, and enlisted their support with promises of an easier, more benevolent rule. To his own followers he promised an equal division of the island's wealth, access to any Indian woman they pleased, and free passage home. Some of the settlers demurred, having an ingrained respect for the authority of their sovereigns' representative. Others, however, who were more adventurous, flocked to Roldan's banner. After all, he was the "alcalde mayor," or chief justice, of the island, and he promised to intervene in their behalf when they eventually returned to Spain.

In 1497, when the adelantado departed for the province of Xaragua to settle a dispute over tribute, Roldan planned to assassinate him. The occasion was to be the execution of one Barahona, a friend of the rebels, who had been tried and convicted for his crimes. Fortunately Bartholomew commuted the death sentence when he returned, so that the assassination plot was aborted. Roldan then planned to seize Fort Conceptión in the province of Cibao, believing that he could subjugate the whole island from that vantage point.

Fort Conceptión had been built by Columbus during the second voyage. It was commanded by Miguel Ballester, a sturdy fighter who was loyal to the Columbus brothers. When Miguel learned of Roldan's plot against the fort, he sent word to Bartholomew and doubled his guard. The adelantado moved quickly and reached the fort with reinforcements before Roldan arrived. To encourage his own men to resist, Bartholomew promised each of them two slaves apiece. Arriving at Concepción to find determined resistance, Roldan decided to talk rather than attack. He asked for the caravel at Isabella; this vessel Diego Columbus had beached high and dry for reasons of safety. Bartholomew refused, pointing out the vessel's poor condition and lack of rigging and the lack of seamen in Roldan's party. The two men parted in anger, and Roldan marched to Isabella, where he plundered the arsenal and storehouse. Then he took his men to the fertile province of Xaragua where there was food and "the best-looking, best-natured women in the country."

This situation lasted for some time, and sentiment for the rebels grew with each passing month of hardship. The fortunate arrival of two relief ships in February, 1498, strengthened Bartholomew's position. The supplies were welcome, of course, but the best news was confirmation of the Admiral's safe arrival in Spain and the king's official approval of Bartholomew as the adelantado of Hispaniola. This official recognition served to stiffen the will of certain "loyalists" who were discontented with Bartholomew's regime and were considering escape to Roldan's group. Royal retribution in those days was harsh and swift. Open rebellion in the face of this news was too risky for most of the men at Santo Domingo, so they remained loyal.

After this good fortune, Bartholomew suffered a reversal. The relief ships of the Admiral's third voyage, which Columbus had ordered to sail directly to Hispaniola while he explored southern waters, missed their landfall and ended up off the coast of Xaragua, well to the south and west of the port. There the unsuspecting sailors met with members of Roldan's party, who came on board under the pretext of friendship. The secret leaked out before the rebels could get their hands on many of the supplies, and the ship's alert captain made haste to sail. Captain Carvajal set his laborers ashore so that they could march overland to Santo Domingo, but, to his surprise, they joined Roldan's rebels. At this, the captains held a quick conference. They decided that Carvajal should remain ashore and attempt to make peace with Roldan, while the other two got all three ships under way for Santo Domingo. The ships' arrival at Santo Domingo after considerable delay and hardship was a disappointment. Most of their provisions had spoiled and Carvajal's ship was leaking so badly that it barely floated. Meanwhile, Captain Carvajal trekked overland to Santo Domingo to report to the Admiral of his experiences with Roldan.

The rebel party grew larger and stronger, having gained recruits from Santo Domingo. By October it was quite evident to the Admiral that he now had the weaker force. If he mustered all able-bodied men his "army" numbered about seventy, and only half of these men were really trustworthy. Columbus therefore decided to swallow his pride and negotiate peace with Roldan. His ultimate aim was to get the rebels out of Hispaniola by promising free passage home. He sent Carvajal and Miguel Ballester into the rebel camp, but all that they got was a letter reply from Roldan to the Admiral, putting all blame for the rebellion on the adelantado.

Columbus had been holding ships in port, hoping that

some of the rebels would take advantage of his offer for passage home. However, the ships were almost filled with slaves, many of whom became ill in their confined quarters on board. On October 18, 1498, the Admiral released the ships and they set sail for Spain. In November, after much jockeying back and forth, the Admiral and Roldan met for a conference. It was a humiliating experience for Columbus, who, with all the power of the throne behind him, faced an insolent rebel who made exorbitant demands. It length the two agreed that the rebels would be pardoned, would receive certificates of good conduct and free passage home, and would be allowed to take their own personal slaves and gold with them. Those who chose to remain on Hispaniola would be given land grants. Columbus agreed to make two caravels ready for sea within 50 days. This last provision was one that he could not meet, so the rebels repudiated their treaty and demanded new negotiations.

This untenable situation dragged on for another year, with Columbus weakening periodically to Roldan's demands. Finally, in October, 1499, he sent Miguel Ballester and Garcia de Barrantes back to plead his case in the Spanish court. They carried letters which enumerated and explained all the concessions made to the rebels, and urged the monarchs to bring the miscreants to trial.

Meanwhile, Columbus faced new difficulties. He received word that strange Spanish caravels were anchored off the western end of Hispaniola, and that landing parties were foraging ashore. He persuaded Roldan that this group represented a common enemy and he pointed out, moreover, that the intruders were poaching in Xaragua, Roldan's beloved province, the home of the rebels. Joined by a common cause, Roldan accosted the strangers under the authority of Christopher Columbus, admiral of the oceans and viceroy of the island. To his surprise he found that the captain-general was none other than Alonso de Hojeda, hero of the second voyage and warrior of renown. Hojeda had, with the consent of Juan de Fonseca, arranged a private voyage for profit into the "Gulf of Pearls" and along the Pearl Coast. He had obtained copies of Columbus' charts and had enlisted the aid of some famous explorers who were unoccupied at the time. In his group there was Juan de la Cosa, the mapmaker, and the Italian navigator, Amerigo Vespucci. The latter's account of this voyage, which he is accused of predating by two years, was so cleverly written that the new continent was eventually named "America" in his honor.

Hojeda's expedition had sailed through the Gulf of Paria to the Pearl Coast on the mainland, which he had named Venezuela. He ran low on provisions, and in spite of Fonseca's warning not to touch any territory discovered by Columbus prior to 1495, he made for Hispaniola, where he knew that he could obtain cassava bread. His men were baking bread and cutting firewood when Roldan accosted them. After several incidents in which Roldan and Hojeda captured each other's men as hostages, the ships finally left.

Roldan and Columbus then worked out an arrangement which led to coexistence, and the two cooperated a second time in putting down a rebellion led by Adrian de Moxica. This revolt was triggered by a young well-born Spaniard's love for a native beauty. Fernando de Guevara, an adventurer whom Columbus had ordered home for his dissolute habits, fell in love with the daughter of Anacaona, one of the great beauties of Xaragua. It is said that Roldan himself was also attracted to the young lady and that he raised every possible obstacle to prevent the wedding. Guevara, a hot-blooded Spaniard, quite naturally formed a plot to kill Roldan. Word leaked out and the young lover was promptly seized and thrown into prison at Santo Domingo. His cousin, Adrian de Moxica, was so enraged at this shabby treatment that he set out through the hills of Hispaniola to enlist the natives' aid in a war of liberation. Before the war could begin, however, Columbus threw aside his role of patient pacifier and moved with vigor to capture Moxica and his principal followers. He executed Moxica promptly and put other ringleaders in chains.

This display of firmness had a remarkable stabilizing effect upon the whole island, and a fairly secure peace pervaded Hispaniola for the first time in years. Despite this accomplishment, Columbus again fell into bad luck. Shortly after he had put down all opposition, Francisco de Bobadilla arrived with full authority to inquire into the affairs of the island and to remove Columbus from the government if the inquiry indicated grave misconduct. Diego Columbus was in command at Santo Domingo when Bobadilla arrived. Christopher and Bartholomew were in the interior of the island. It was most unfortunate timing. Seven ringleaders of the Moxica rebellion had just been hanged and five more were in prison awaiting execution. Bobadilla was enraged to find that "the foreigners" were shedding Spanish blood. Without any inquiry, he jumped to the conclusion that the Columbus brothers were indeed a cruel, bloodthirsty lot who should be removed to Spain for trial. Accordingly he imprisoned Diego, seized control of the government, and freed the remaining prisoners. When Columbus, in answer to a summons, returned to Santo Domingo, Bobadilla imprisoned him and bound the dignified Admiral with chains. Bartholomew received the same treatment. All three were put aboard a ship sailing for Spain in October, 1500.

Bobadilla had gone too far. The sight of the stately Admiral in chains at Cádiz created a wave of sympathy among the populace. The rabble might call him "Admiral of the mosquitoes" and jeer, but the average Spaniard was outraged. Here was the man whose discovery in 1492 launched Spain on the path to world glory. His previous returns had been exciting parades which made the people proud to be Spanish subjects. This was shameful treatment, no matter how poorly he had governed the new settlement. Fonseca sensed this public opinion and wisely made no effort to capitalize on Columbus' bad fortune. In December, King Ferdinand and Queen Isabella ordered the Admiral's release and summoned him to court. There, in a touching interview in which both the queen and Columbus were in tears, the sovereigns forgave the great explorer, and promised to restore his income and rights.

PART V

Fourth Voyage

CHAPTER 14

SPAIN, 1500-1502

HAVING been absolved of all charges against him, Christopher Columbus felt a great surge of hope. In his mind's eye he envisioned a triumphant return to Hispaniola, armed with due authority to punish his accusers. Unfortunately, however, he was pushed into the background by more urgent matters of state, and indeed became relegated to the fringes of the court for a year and a half, awaiting a revival of the royal interest. These must have been frustrating years for the aging Admiral. Great voyages of discovery were making news frequently and for him time was running out.

Portugal's star rose when Vasco da Gama returned to Lisbon in 1499 with news of a sea route to the Indies. His ships were loaded with pearls, spices, silks, and other cargo. By comparison, this profitable voyage made the Spanish discoveries in the New World seem unimportant. Shortly afterward, another Portuguese mariner, Pedro Cabral, managed to touch the coast of Brazil when he was blown to the west of the normal sailing route to the Cape of Good Hope. Cabral landed near the harbor of Porto Seguro in 1500 and claimed that land for Portugal. At about this same time, Vicente

Yanez Pinzón coasted the shores of Brazil and discovered the mouth of the Amazon River. By far the most profitable Spanish voyage of the time was that of Pedro Alonso Niño. He followed Hojeda to the Venezuelan Pearl Coast on a private voyage and returned with a fortune in pearls. His was the first Spanish voyage to the New World that proved to be extremely profitable.

Needless to say, these were unhappy months for the Admiral. He had shown the way, and now dozens of other mariners were profiting from his initial achievement. King Ferdinand, realizing that he had made a great mistake in granting so much authority to Columbus on the first voyage, conveniently looked the other way. He decided to keep Columbus out of island administration permanently, and sent Nicholas de Ovando to Hispaniola to relieve Bobadilla. In September, 1501, however, he issued a royal decree authorizing restoration of all property that had been taken from the Admiral, and gave him permission to send a factor (representative) with the next fleet to look after his interests. To the penniless Columbus, who had been living on the charity of friends for a year, this was consolation at last. While he resented the loss of his title of governor and viceroy of the islands, his fortune at least had been returned to him.

On February 13, 1502, Ovando sailed from Cádiz with a large fleet and a brilliant entourage. Aboard the 30 ships there were 2,500 sailors and passengers—hidalgos, colonists with their famliies, and trained men-at-arms. Ferdinand and Isabella had finally learned that pardoned convicts were not good material for the establishment of a colony in the New World. This time they sent a number of wellborn citizens of rank, and a group of respectable married men with their families.

Meanwhile, Columbus was busily writing out his "Book of Privileges," which he hoped would be useful to his family in eventually reclaiming all that he had once been granted. At the same time, he saw fit to compose a wandering and vague religious paper which predicted the end of the world. This study stressed the importance of another crusade to conquer the Holy Land—an obsession he had cherished since his first voyage.

From this work he hit upon the idea of one last great voyage of discovery. Realizing that the coasts of both North America and South America were becoming fairly well defined, he proposed to push through the Caribbean Sea and once more seek a westward passage through what is now called Central America. To his surprise, this proposal was well received by the sovereigns, who, it is presumed, were more than happy to foot the bill in order to have their "admiral of the oceans" at sea rather than at court.

The royal instructions for this fourth voyage urged Columbus to "set sail speedily." The monarchs were loath to have him appear at Hispaniola and specifically forbade it on the outward voyage. They would, however, permit him to touch there for a short time during the return passage if it became necessary. In order to preserve the good relations that then existed between Spain and Portugal, they gave Columbus a blanket letter of introduction to the captain of the Portuguese fleet, explaining that he was sailing westward to the Orient. A hint of their hopes to find a passage appears in the next phrase of the letter. The monarchs stated that they had learned that Portuguese ships were sailing eastward for the same destination, and hoped that the two expeditions might meet at sea. Should this occur, they wished fervently that each would treat the other with courtesy and friendship.

Columbus was pleased to obtain permission to take his young son, Ferdinand, with him. The lad was only 13 years old, but he had keen powers of observation and an excellent memory. Ferdinand's description of this fourth voyage is by far the most interesting and vivid account of the Admiral that has survived. Bartholomew, his trusted brother (still adelantado of Hispaniola in name if not in fact), was also permitted to sail on the voyage. At Queen Isabella's order, Columbus was forbidden to traffic in slaves. She had never acquiesced to his previous slave practices, and she was practical enough to note how badly the poor creatures fared in the strange climate and surroundings of Spain. As for other things of value, "gold, silver, pearls and precious stones," the sovereigns installed a member of the court, Francisco de Porras, as their business representative. He was to take custody of all such valuable cargo and prepare suitable ledgers and accounts. As a last precaution, Arabic interpreters were provided in the event that the Admiral found his passage and made contact with the Great Khan of Cathay.

At this time, Columbus was not so physically strong as he had been on his previous trips. The years of exposure and hardship had taken their toll; he suffered from arthritis and his vision was failing. Yet his mind was still active and he was still without a peer at dead-reckoning sailing and seamanship. As his writing indicates, he had frequent visions, and was also on the verge of becoming a religious fanatic. But in spite of these drawbacks, the old Admiral acquitted himself well, and in his declining years he referred to this fourth voyage as his favorite.

CHAPTER 15

"GRACIAS A DIOS"

IN the spring of 1502, Columbus completed his treatise on religious prophecies and settled his business affairs to his satisfaction. Pleased with these accomplishments, he then began preparations for the voyage. "In this," Ferdinand wrote, "he showed such diligence that in a short time he had rigged and made ready four ships with roundtops, the largest one being of seventy tons burthen, and the smallest of fifty tons, with one hundred and forty men and boys all told, myself being one." The four ships, all caravels, were named *La Capitana, La Gallega, Bermuda,* and *Vizcaina.* While these sturdy vessels served him well, not one survived the hardships of the fourth voyage, which was by far the most difficult and trying of all the Admiral's sea adventures.

Columbus got under way from the harbor of Cádiz on May 9 and anchored near Santa Catalina, an old castle that guarded the port. He took final departure two days later, and set a course for the coast of Morocco, where the Moors were reported to have attacked the Portuguese at Arzila. This was young Ferdinand's first adventure, for he was allowed to accompany the adelantado ashore. The Moors had withdrawn before the fleet arrived, so the landing turned out to be only a courtesy call. The wounded Portuguese captain of the fort was grateful for this gesture of aid, and sent a group of his officers to make a return call on Columbus. Some of these gentlemen turned out to have been cousins of Dona Felipa de Moniz, the Admiral's deceased wife. After an exchange of pleasantries, Columbus sailed before sunset, satisfied that the day had helped to cement good relations between Spain and Portugal.

The ships reached the Grand Canary on May 20 and anchored for four days off Las Palmas. Columbus then shifted berths to Maspalomas to gather wood and to fill his water kegs with fresh water. With these chores out of the way, he got under way on the night of the 25th and set course "for the Indies." This must have been one of the Admiral's most pleasant crossings, for Ferdinand reports it as a "prosperous voyage." They arrived at the island of Martinique on June 15 "without having to touch sails." Here they rested for three days while the men bathed, washed their clothes, and replenished the ship's supply of wood and fresh water.

These were familiar waters. Nine years before, during his second voyage, Columbus had explored this chain of beautiful islands while en route to Hispaniola. This time he followed the same general route, sailing northwest along the chain to St. Croix, then passing south of Puerto Rico to make a landfall on the eastern tip of Hispaniola. It was easy sailing; the winds were favorable, the weather was pleasant, and the "islands of the sun" were lush and green. The fleet arrived off Santo Domingo on June 29, just a few jumps ahead of a seasonal hurricane that was making up behind them.

Their arrival marked the end of pleasantry; from this point on, the fourth voyage became a trial in which both man and the elements seemed to oppose every move that Columbus made.

Some of Columbus' troubles were no doubt self-inflicted. For example, he had no business being at Santo Domingo; his instructions specifically forbade him to stop at Hispaniola on the outward leg of the voyage. Yet here he was, just two months after Ovando had relieved Bobadilla as governor. He gave as his excuse a desire to trade one of his ships, the *Bermuda*, which had proved to be "a dull sailer." (It is difficult to believe that experienced old mariners like Columbus and Bartholomew could be hoodwinked into chartering an unseaworthy ship.) Despite this professed reason, it is more likely that Columbus was at Santo Domingo out of curiosity. All of his fortune had been taken from him by Bobadilla two years earlier, but now the Admiral's representative was in the settlement to recapture it.

When he arrived off the entrance to Santo Domingo, Columbus saw the signs of bad weather coming on. He sent one of his captains, Pedro de Terreros, ashore to explain the reason for his presence and to request permission to enter the harbor to take shelter from the hurricane. Governor Ovando refused the Admiral's request and ignored his warning of a great storm.

Ovando had been busy since his arrival at Santo Domingo in April. To impress his sovereigns back home, he had loaded 28 ships with valuable cargo and "time-expired men" who longed for the sight of Spain and a taste of civilization. The flagship is reported to have carried 200,000 castellanos' worth of gold, including a tremendous nugget that a native woman had found in a stream. All told, the combined cargo represented the greatest wealth ever sent back to Spain from Hispaniola. Many of the Admiral's old enemies, including Bobadilla and Roldan, were aboard the ships. Although Columbus did not know it, the smallest and "meanest" ship of this fleet, the *Aguja*, carried 4,000 pesos of gold in his name. This was the amount that Ovando had given the Admiral's factor as lost revenues that had been withheld by Bobadilla.

The fleet was about to sail when Columbus arrived with his prophetic warning. Nevertheless, the ships got under way at Ovando's order and disdainfully stood past Columbus and out to sea. The Admiral noted Ovando's refusal and turned his attention to his own ships. Having ridden out hurricanes before, he sought shelter west of the city, and anchored close to some headlands that protected a small cove. Here they rode out the early part of the hurricane, but on the night of June 30 three of the caravels parted their anchor cables and were forced to put to sea in order to ride out the storm. *La Capitana*'s anchor held, and Columbus "saved his ship by lying close to shore, like a sage astrologer who foresaw whence the danger must come." *La Gallega*, *Bermuda*, and *Vizcaina* survived in deep water, although they took great punishment. All four rendezvoused the following Sunday in the harbor of Azua, on the southern coast of Hispaniola. Columbus described the storm as follows: "The tempest was terrible throughout the night, all the ships were separated, and each one driven to the last extremity, without hope of anything but death, each of them also looked upon the loss of the rest as a matter of certainty." But, he concluded, "The Lord restored them to me in His own good time."

Meanwhile, Ovando's fleet had reached the eastern tip of Hispaniola when the hurricane struck. The flagship, with Bobadilla and Roldan aboard, went down with all hands. Others were either sunk or driven ashore, where huge waves pounded them to pieces. Only a few managed to return to Santo Domingo, too badly battered to attempt a crossing without extensive repairs. It has been estimated that 500 lives and 19 ships were lost in this disaster. By sheer luck, the only ship of the entire fleet to weather the storm and make it back to Spain was none other than the *Aguja*, the one carrying Columbus' gold. Ferdinand writes of this poetic justice, "The Admiral's enemies charged that by his magic arts he had raised the storm to take revenge on Bobadilla and others of his enemies who were with him . . . not one of his four ships went down, while of the twenty-eight which had left with Bobadilla, only one, and that one of the meanest, the *Aguja*, reached Spain safely. . . ."

The Admiral rested in Azua for several days while the crews repaired torn rigging, bathed, and fished. One day a fishing party in *Vizcaina's* boat came upon a sea ray "as large as a medium sized bed" sleeping on the surface. They harpooned him so firmly that they were towed about the harbor by the powerful fish at great speed. They finally killed the ray and hoisted it aboard ship with a heavy tackle, so that all could see their strange catch. Ferdinand writes of another strange "fish" —a manatee, which is a mammal whose appearance has often caused seamen to report it as a mermaid. Ferdinand said that it was as big as a calf and that "it resembled one in taste and color."

The ships sailed from Azua a few days later, and once more Columbus saw signs of an approaching storm. He put in at Puerto Brazil (now Jacmel) and waited until July 14 before venturing out to sea again. This time he headed west toward the place where he hoped to find the elusive strait to the Indies. Off Jamaica he ran into a flat calm that left the ships helpless, with sails hanging limply against the masts. Here the current carried them slightly northwest and toward the Queen's Garden off the southern coast of Cuba. The Admiral anchored off one of the islets for several days, waiting for a fair wind. Soon the easterly trades set in and the ships made excellent time on a westerly heading, reaching Bay Islands off the coast of Honduras on July 30. Bartholomew took a small landing party ashore at the island of Bonacca, but found very little of interest. The natives were slightly different from others that the Spaniards had seen—Ferdinand observed that they had "narrower foreheads."

At this point they encountered a very large native canoe, "long as a galley and eight feet wide," which was loaded with merchandise. The canoe's 25 paddlers were not afraid of the strangers, and drew their canoe alongside *La Capitana* to trade. Columbus was impressed to find cotton mantles, sleeveless shirts, wooden swords, flint knives, copper hatchets, and even a passable wine. The natives used "almonds" (cacao beans) for currency. During this exchange, Columbus noted that the women kept their faces covered and that they were as modest as the Moorish women of Granada. The canoe had come from the north, possibly from some section of Yucatán, but Columbus chose not to follow it back home. Instead he wished to continue his search for the strait, and reasoned that it was to the south. However, the coast of Honduras at this point runs east-west, and the Admiral had to face a significant problem of seamanship before he could get farther south. He had to beat his way east against both wind and current—a feat almost beyond the capacity of the caravels. Taking an older native with him as an interpreter, Columbus made the short run to the Honduras coast. Bartholomew landed and took possession of the country on August 17.

The long beat to windward was a trial for the aging Admiral, who, crippled with an attack of arthritis, directed operations from a covered couch on the quarterdeck. Day after day went by without any cessation of rain, thunder, or lightning. Columbus writes of this weary voyage with clarity. He "saw neither sun nor stars" during this "fearful tempest" and his ships "lay exposed, with sails torn, and anchors, rigging, cables, boats and a great quantity of provisions lost." His crew, he wrote, "were very weak and humbled in spirit, many of them promising to lead a religious life, and all making vows and promising to perform pilgrimages." Some of them would "go to their messmates to make confession."

Throughout this ordeal the Admiral noted with pride that young Ferdinand more than carried his load. He endured the toil with such strength that he encouraged others and "worked as if he had been eighty years at sea."

On September 14 the stubborn Admiral had his reward—the coast took a southerly trend. This meant an end of crawling, and fair sailing once again. With a fervent sincerity, he named the turning point Cape Gracias a Dios (Thanks to God).

CHAPTER 16

THE MOSQUITO COAST

IF Columbus had known that he would spend the next seven months off this mosquito-ridden coast searching for his strait and for gold, he probably would have returned promptly to Hispaniola. But he was as stubborn an elderly explorer as he had been a younger one. During this period he lost many good sailors and two ships, and he failed to find the strait. (Ferdinand asserts that he did—that some straits are "land" and some are "water.")

Not long after the Admiral cruised the Atlantic coasts of Nicaragua, Costa Rica, and Panama, Vasco Nuñez de Balboa crossed the isthmus and discovered the Pacific Ocean on the other side. Ferdinand claims that the route of the mule trains along which the gold of the Incas was shipped across Panama represented a "strait" whose discovery resulted from Columbus' fourth voyage. . . .

This portion of the voyage was exasperating and frustrating. Admittedly, it began with easier sailing. Once the ships rounded Cape Gracias a Dios they made excellent time south. On September 16 they reached the mouth of a river that has been identified as either the Rio Grande or the Bluefields, both of which are in Nicaragua. Columbus decided to send boats upriver for wood and water, but as they reached the bar, a heavy sea built up and one of the craft was swamped. Two men drowned in the riptide, causing the Admiral to name the river Rio de Los Desastres.

Continuing southward, the ships reached Puerto Limón, Costa Rica, where the Admiral brought them to anchor off a beautiful island which he named La Huerta (The Garden). They spent several days trying to trade with Indians who came out in great numbers from the mainland. Columbus tried a new stratagem— he forbade his men to take any native goods in return for the usual hawk's bells and other trading junk carried for barter. At this, the Indians refused to give up their own goods, suspecting that Spaniards were sorcerers. The Indians then tried a new gambit of their own. Holding aloft a signal of truce, an old man boarded *La Capitana* to make the ship a gift of two young maidens, one eight and the other fourteen years old. The girls showed no fright and, according to Ferdinand, were quite maidenly. Columbus gave orders that they should not be harmed, dressed them, and put them ashore with a load of trinkets. Here again his strategy backfired. The old native was glad to have the girls back, but they left all of the Admiral's gifts on the beach. Now neither side trusted the other.

Bartholomew, the adelantado, went ashore to question some of the chiefs about their country, taking along a secretary to make notes. When the conference began and the secretary took out his pen and paper, the Indians became frightened. They fled into the woods and could only be induced to return when their medicine men had scattered powder into the air to offset the Europeans' "magic."

This sort of cat-and-mouse play proceeded without result until October 2, when the Admiral decided to send an armed party ashore. The Spaniards looked around at will, noting that the area abounded with game. They found an interesting burial ground and a few strange animals such as a spider monkey, but there was really nothing of value anywhere. Satisfied at last, Columbus put his rested men to work. They seized two natives as guides and got under way on October 5.

As they moved south, the Admiral explored every indentation of the coast. They entered a large bay with eager anticipation but soon found it to be land-blocked, and not the strait that they were searching for. Yet here, at last, the natives ashore wore golden ornaments. As usual these Indians would trade for trifles, so the explorers set out for gold in earnest. The first villagers kept pointing south (toward Veragua) as the place where the gold was mined.

Since it became more evident each day that the search for a strait was going badly, the Admiral instead turned his thoughts and energies toward gold. A cargo of this precious metal would be well received back in Spain, and it would quiet inquisitive tongues. Actually, from a practical point of view, this fourth voyage had yielded little and there was very little time left. Sea worms, the dreaded *teredos*, were wreaking havoc below the waterline; the ships' rigging and sails were patchwork; and provisions were running low. In the remaining time available to him, Columbus determined to make the

voyage a financial success. On October 17 he reached
the coast of Veragua—the Central American province
which eventually passed to his heirs. The trade in gold
was brisk and profitable, but the Admiral would not
tarry as long as there was another horizon to cross.
From Veragua onward, the Spaniards found the Indians
to be more warlike and less frightened of intruders. It
became necessary to fire warning shots at the shore
before the natives could be induced to trade.

By November 2 he reached a fine port close to the
present entrance to the Panama Canal. Because of its
beautiful groves and fruits he named it Porto Bello, and
settled down happily for a few days' rest in these pleasant surroundings. Moving eastward, he rounded Cape
Nombre de Dios and took shelter from bad weather in
a small cove. The ships were moored so close to shore
that the sailors found it easy to take "French leave" at
night. They acted so badly ashore, being "a greedy and
dissolute set of men," that they provoked the Indians to
battle. The Admiral finally had to fire a shot into a group
of them before he could restore peace. Afterward there
was little contact, and consequently almost no opportunity to trade. Columbus decided to return to Veragua,
where he had found more gold than at any other place,
to search again for the fabled gold mines.

He started back on December 5 and ran headlong
into some of the worst weather of his long experience.
The lightning, thunder, torrential rain, and high winds
kept the Admiral in a sea "which seemed . . . as a sea
of blood, seething in a cauldron on a mighty fire. Never
did the sky look more fearful," he continued, "during
one day and one night it burned like a furnace, and
every instant I looked to see if my masts and my sails

were not destroyed; for the lightnings flashed with such alarming fury that we all thought the ships must have been consumed."

Forced back to their original cove, the crews rested as well as they could before trying the open sea again. In early January, 1503, the battered ships, manned by weak crews, sailed back to Veragua and anchored near the mouth of Rio Belen. Even the most experienced seamen believed that they had selected a safe anchorage, but a little later the Rio Belen proved to be completely unpredictable. It suddenly flooded to a great height, snapping *La Capitana*'s anchor cable, and driving her into a collision with *Gallega*. When he finally brought order out of this new chaos, Columbus summed up the entire experience with "I do not know if anyone else ever suffered greater trials."

He now began to search for gold in earnest. Bartholomew took the ships' boats down the coast and ascended the Veragua River in search of gold mines. A local native chieftain named Quibian freely volunteered directions. This puzzled Columbus, until he found out that the crafty Quibian had given directions to the mines of a rival chief. Bartholomew's men accumulated a good supply of gold during this foray. They traded for golden medals and they dug gold out of the earth with their bare hands and with knives. In other explorations in Veragua they were similarly succesful. These adventures proved so profitable that the Admiral decided to found a settlement there. In this decision the old mariner was blinded by his desire for gold. This section of Veragua was so wild and inhospitable that it never has been properly settled even to this day. Nevertheless, there was gold in the steaming jungle, and Columbus was determined to make this a profitable voyage. He intended to build a settlement and then make a quick round trip to Spain for more supplies. Brother Bartholomew, a tower of strength in times like these, would remain behind. Columbus blithely ignored the fact that they were settling on a hostile coast, and forgot the terrible example of Navidad, the first settlement in Hispaniola, which was completely wiped out during a year's absence of the Spanish caravels.

The natives watched the construction of houses for a settlement in silent hatred. Soon cacique Quibian formed a federation devoted to the expulsion of the Spaniards. Columbus learned of these plans through the daring services of Diego Mendez, a capable gentleman-soldier who was absolutely fearless. He ventured into the camps and war councils of the Indians, discovered their plans, and reported everything to the Admiral. Mendez proposed a scheme to capture Quibian in order to counter the Indian war plans. He took a group of men upriver and captured the Indian leader and most of his family. During the return trip downriver, however, the wily Quibian persuaded one of his guards to loosen his bonds, which, he complained, were inhumanly tight. Shortly afterward, the cacique slipped over the boat's side and disappeared into the night. He was presumed to have drowned until he was seen much later leading an attack on the adelantado's camp. This occurred in April, just before Columbus was preparing to get his ships under way.

The hardy Spaniards repelled the attack even though they were outnumbered twenty to one. With the assistance of one fierce bloodhound they inflicted numerous casualties on their attackers, while suffering only a few minor wounds themselves. Shortly thereafter, a watering party led by Diego Tristan was ambushed at the river's edge and all but one man was killed. This success inspired the natives to greater efforts against Bartholomew's settlement. The woods afforded shelter right up to the limits of the settlement buildings, and soon a great mass of Indians howled down on the camp. Their yells and fierce gestures unnerved the defenders, who speedily saw the folly of being abandoned on this hostile shore. They sent word to Columbus on board *La Capitana* not to sail without them. Their case was hopeless, they said, and the only possible solution was to abandon the fort as soon as possible.

A gusty wind and high surf at the bar prevented any immediate action, so Columbus had to wait for several anxious days. During this interval some captive Indians escaped from the ship's hold. Others who were restrained hanged themselves during the night. At this demonstration of determination Columbus almost despaired. It was at this terrible moment that he believed that he spoke with God for guidance. In his letter to Ferdinand and Isabella, he described the event as follows: "I was alone, outside, upon that dangerous coast, suffering from a severe fever and worn with fatigue. All hope of escape was gone. I toiled up to the highest part of the ship, and, with a quivering voice and fast-falling tears, I called upon your Highnesses' war captains from each point of the compass to come to my succor, but there was no reply. At length, groaning with exhaustion, I fell asleep, and heard a compassionate voice address me thus—'O fool, and slow to believe and to serve thy God, the God of all! What did he do for Moses or for David, His servants, than He has done for thee . . . Thine old age shall not prevent thee from any great undertaking . . . Fear not and trust; all these tribulations are recorded on marble, and not without cause.' "

Thus encouraged, the infirm Admiral stuck it out, and waited for better weather. The men in the fort then floated out their belongings on rafts, and soon crossed the bar themselves by this means. The men crowded into three ships, for Columbus had decided to abandon *La Gallega*, which by now was little more than a worm-eaten hulk. Never did a group quit a harbor with such rejoicing; it was three weeks before they actually cleared the "mosquito coast," but the first move away from Veragua was welcome to all.

Columbus sailed east on April 16, despite grumbling by his crews, who felt that the course homeward was to the north. But the old explorer was covering his tracks. He was able to say of his crew, "None of them can explain whither I went, nor whence I came." And, he added, "They can give no other account than that they went to lands where there was an abundance of gold, and this they can certify surely enough; but they do not know the way to return thither for such a purpose; they would be obliged to go on a voyage of discovery as much as if they had never been there before." Apparently the Admiral had had enough poaching in "his" Caribbean. Many adventurers were willing to follow his tracks on voyages of profit. He remembered only too well how Hojeda and Niño had been first to exploit the riches of the Pearl Coast of Venezuela in 1499.

Bad weather and the poor condition of his ships held him back. He put in to Porto Bello and there abandoned the *Vizcaina*, another victim of sea worms. The remaining two ships were barely afloat, and were kept buoyant only by incessant pumping day and night. Columbus continued eastward along the northern coast of Panama until May 1, and then steered north toward Cuba and Hispaniola. His point of departure was just east of the Gulf of Darien. He sought shelter from a storm in the lee of an island in the Queen's Garden, south of Cuba, and pushed on. Progress was slow as the water-laden caravels were fighting both wind and current. By the middle of June they were almost in sight of Haiti, but could go no farther east. In order to save his crew, Columbus changed course for Jamaica, and beached the two ships in St. Ann's Bay on June 25.

His glorious fourth voyage of discovery was over. He had abandoned two ships and had now beached the remaining two. The Admiral's voyage now became a problem of survival until help came. If he and his men had perished on Jamaica, the fruits of their toil along the Mosquito Coast and the secret of the gold mines in Veragua would have been buried with them.

The men built shelters on the decks of the *Bermuda* and *Capitana* and lashed the two ships together. They shored up the rotting timbers, and, thanking God that at least they were not in a watery grave, sent messengers to look about the land for food.

CHAPTER 17

BEACHCOMBERS

COLUMBUS was so ill with arthritis that he was bed-ridden during the entire sojourn at Jamaica, which lasted almost one year. But his iron will still dominated the band of 116 men and boys. Fearing the retribution that would surely come if he loosed his crew on the island, he kept the entire group aboard the unique fortress and granted shore leaves to only a few at a time.

Ferdinand assures us that the sailors were "by nature disrespectful," and that "no punishment or order could have stopped them from running about the country and into the Indians' huts to steal what they found and commit outrages on their wives and children. . . ." This had happened before on the Mosquito Coast of Central America where the expedition had ships as a means to escape retaliation. Here in Jamaica they were marooned high and dry in two rotting ships' hulks, beached a short distance from the shore. The Admiral knew how tenuous his position was, and almost immediately conceived a plan for rescue.

However, food was the most immediate problem, so he sent his trusted and able captain, Diego Mendez, ashore with three companions to trade with the natives for provisions. Later, in 1536, when the aging Diego Mendez was dictating his last will and testament to a notary in Santo Domingo, he included an account of his services with "the very illustrious Admiral Don Christopher Columbus, of glorious memory." Referring to the ordeal at Jamaica, Mendez noted that he had given out the last ration of biscuit and wine shortly after the ships had arrived. Then, he said, "I took my sword in hand, three men only accompanying me, and advanced into the island." He found that the local natives were friendly and cheerful, and he easily persuaded them to contract for a supply of food. In return for their efforts they would be paid in "blue beads, combs and knives, hawks' bells and fish hooks." At each of three villages Mendez made these arrangements, sending back one of his men each time to inform Columbus of their progress. Eventually Mendez proceeded alone toward the eastern end of the island, where he boldly entered a village by himself. Mendez proved to be a great salesman; in a short time he and the local chief became blood brothers. After a rest with his new friend, Mendez bought a canoe and returned to Columbus with six Indian paddlers. At the sight of this canoe, loaded to the gunwales with provisions, Columbus was overjoyed. He hobbled out on the quarterdeck to embrace Diego Mendez and to thank God for his safe return.

The provision contracts began well. Indians came daily to trade and there was ample food. Some Spanish stomachs rebelled at the new diet, but the threat of famine disappeared. Columbus now turned to the problem of getting word to Santo Domingo, the nearest port where a relief expedition could be organized. The only feasible means was to wait for a period of calm and send a canoe across the 108 miles that separate Jamaica and Haiti. This would be perilous, with little chance for success, but he had to try. The Jamaican canoe was little more than a primitive hollowed-out log with very little freeboard.

The Admiral first approached Diego Mendez, whose courage and reliability had been tested before. Even the redoubtable Mendez was hesitant, saying, "My Lord, I have many times put my life in danger to save yours, and the lives of all those who are with you, and God has marvelously preserved me: In consequence of this, there have not been wanting murmurers who have said that your lordship entrusts every honorable undertaking to me, while there are others amongst them who would perform them as well as I." He then suggested that Columbus assemble all hands and ask for volunteers. If none appeared, Diego agreed to try.

As he expected, not a man stepped forward, so Mendez volunteered. Columbus then composed a letter to his sovereigns which he gave to Diego Mendez for delivery at first opportunity. Surprisingly, this letter, which one would think would have been lost, is one of the better pieces of evidence that survived the fourth voyage. Now called the *Lettera Rarissima*, this is a dignified but pathetic account of suffering and exploration.

Mendez pulled his canoe up on the shore to prepare it for the long voyage. He was a good seaman and he knew what to do. He fixed a false keel to the bottom and "pitched and greased it." Next he "nailed some boards upon the poop and prow, to prevent the sea from coming in . . . fixed a mast in it, set up a sail, and laid in the necessary provisions." Mendez' first attempt failed. Although he made it to the eastern end of Jamaica, he went ashore for fresh water and was captured by unfriendly Indian "pirates." His captors began casting lots for his life and the canoe, forgetting him momentarily. This was all that Mendez needed. He slipped away, returned to his canoe, and sailed back to the ships at St. Ann's Bay.

He asked for an armed force to accompany him to the island's end for protection. Bartholomew Columbus took a group of 70 men to assure a safe departure. Mendez and Bartolomeo Fieschi, "a Genoese gentleman," took two canoes, "each taking a crew of six Christians and ten Indian paddlers." Columbus instructed Mendez to proceed to Santo Domingo after the crossing. There he was to organize and send out a rescue party to Jamaica while he himself went on to Spain to report to the court. Fieschi would return to Jamaica by canoe to inform the Admiral that everything had worked as planned.

Ferdinand gives a graphic account of the passage, based on interviews he obtained months later with some of the survivors. The Indians paddled, the "Christians" stood guard over the paddlers, and the captain steered. It was rough going against both wind and current. With constant paddling the small canoes made only 30 miles a day. However, they carelessly drank up most of the water supply the first day, and from then on everyone suffered intense thirst. After three days' torture they made the small island of Navassa, thirty miles from the coast of Haiti. There they rested, quenched their thirst, and ate shellfish. Fearing the onset of rough weather, Mendez forced his men back into the canoe that night, and completed the last leg to Cape San Miguel (Tiburon).

Fieschi could not persuade any of his men to attempt the return trip, and few could blame them. Mendez pushed along the south coast of Hispaniola toward Santo Domingo, but learned that the island governor, Ovando, was on a punitive expedition into the province of Xaragua. He, too, set out inland and joined Ovando on the road to Xaragua. The governor kept Mendez with him for seven months, "until he had burned and hanged eighty-four caciques, lords of vassals, and with them Nacaona, the Sovereign mistress of the island."

When the expedition against the natives was over, Mendez walked to Santo Domingo—more than two hundred miles—and waited for some ships to arrive from Spain. In May, 1504, he finally chartered a caravel and sent it to Jamaica, loaded with "provisions, bread, wine, meat, hogs, sheep and fruit." This accomplished, the adventurous Mendez sailed to Spain and sought an audience with the king and queen.

If Mendez was the first hero of Jamaica, Bartholomew Columbus was certainly the second. The Admiral leaned heavily on his fearless brother during the long ordeal in St. Ann's Bay. Fortunately, the adelantado was as great a warrior as he was a sailor. And Columbus needed physical prowess to survive a mutiny in Jamaica. As weeks went by without any word from Mendez and Fieschi, the confines of the stranded ships became unbearable to about half the crew. Many became sick, and others looked longingly at the beautiful shore where there were food, adventure, and women. Soon the brothers Porras, one a ship captain and the other the fleet comptroller, organized forty-eight men to take command from Columbus. On January 2, 1504, the armed mutineers took complete charge. Only the quick thinking of Columbus' servants prevented a massacre.

They kept the ailing Admiral in his cabin, and dis-armed Bartholomew Columbus, who had rushed on deck with a lance, ready to fight the whole pack. Pushing the adelantado into a cabin, the servants then persuaded the Porras brothers to take what they wanted and to depart.

Many others joined the mutineers when they took ten canoes and set out "for Castile." These men were not part of the original mutiny, but they were "desperate at the thought of being abandoned." Columbus was left with a few loyal sailors, plus a number of the sick who were in no condition to leave. Francisco Porras led his motley group to the eastern tip of the island, stopping occasionally to descend on a native village to steal and commit other outrages. When they set out for Hispaniola with Indian captives as paddlers, the weather was fair. But the sea became rough about fifteen miles out, so they turned back. Water came in over the gun-wales of the overloaded canoes, and the frightened Spaniards threw their native paddlers into the sea. When these poor wretches became tired and grasped the sides of the canoes, Spanish swordsmen cut off their hands. Ferdinand says that they killed 18 in this manner, keeping only a few needed to steer.

The mutineers waited for calm weather and tried the passage again. After two more attempts had failed, they gave up and decided to live off the land, moving west-ward slowly back toward the fortress of St. Ann's Bay.

Bartholomew and the Admiral had expected this turn of events. In the interim they had nursed the sick back to health and now commanded a respectable body of men, just about equal in number to the mutineers. They now faced new problems with the Indians, who were growing tired of the provision contracts. With food supplies dwindling, and the natives growing more hostile, something drastic had to be done. The fertile mind of Columbus hit upon an idea.

His almanacs showed that within three days there would be an eclipse of the moon. He sent word to all important chieftains to come to St. Ann's Bay for a conference. To the assembled group the distinguished old Admiral was an impressive figure. He warned them that he was angry at their new attitude and at their failure to deliver provisions. Unless they changed, he said, the next moon would rise inflamed with wrath, signifying God's displeasure. When the moon rose the next evening the eclipse began. The Indians became so frightened that there was "great howling and lamentation" as they came running from all directions to bring food to the ships. The Indians begged Columbus to save them. With that the Admiral retired to his cabin until the eclipse began to wane, and then he came out to announce that his God would forgive the Indians if they would live in friendship and provide provisions in the future. "From that time forward," writes Ferdinand, "they were diligent in providing us with all we needed, and were loud in praise of the Christian God."

In late March, the group was cheered at the sudden appearance of a small caravel. To their bitter disappointment the ship was calling under Ovando's orders to ascertain the condition of Columbus and his men, not to rescue them. The ship's captain, Diego de Escobar, was not one of the Admiral's admirers. He stopped briefly, informed Columbus of the safety of Diego Mendez, and assured him that help would come. He delivered a slab of salt pork and some wine as gifts from Ovando, and promptly departed.

With this news of impending rescue, Columbus tried to patch things up with the mutineers. He sent emissaries to arrange terms with Porras, but they were unsuccessful. In late May, the mutineers marched toward the ships, confident that they could overwhelm the defenders. They were met by Bartholomew Columbus at the head of fifty healthy men. The adelantado loved a good fight, and had survived many in his day. He "fell on his enemies so fiercely" that they soon suffered many casualties. Francisco Porras was made prisoner and the other surviving mutineers ran away. The adelantado would have chased them down, but his lieutenants pointed out that the natives, who had been watching the whole affair with interest, might attack both groups if more Spaniards were killed off.

Ferdinand gives a vivid account of the fate of Pedro de Ledesma, a mutineer who was carved up badly. He had fallen over a cliff out of sight, and only the Indians knew his location. They were curious about the damage caused by Spanish swords, so they opened up Pedro's wounds with little sticks. "He had a cut on the head so deep that one could see his brains," say Ferdinand. There were other wounds, too, one "on the shoulder, which was almost severed, so that his arm hung limp; one thigh was cut to the bone down to the shin bone, and the sole of one foot was sliced from heel to toe so that it resembled a slipper." The loyalists found Ledesma and carried him back to the ships, where he recovered.

Shortly after the bloody fight, the caravel chartered by Mendez arrived. Columbus crowded all hands into the ship and set sail on June 28 for Santo Domingo. Contrary winds and current plagued them en route and slowed their passage. They arrived on August 13, 1504, where they were greeted coolly but courteously by Governor Ovando. In a month Columbus was ready to sail for Spain. The return voyage was rough and the ship almost foundered, but the skill of Bartholomew and Christopher prevailed. They arrived at Sanlucar de Barrameda on November 7, 1504, almost two months after leaving Santo Domingo.

It was a sad homecoming for Columbus. His benefactor and supporter through the years, Queen Isabella, was deathly ill. She died on November 26, leaving the Admiral to face unsympathetic King Ferdinand alone. The tired old sailor spent the winter in Seville, writing letters to his son Diego and other friends in court, pointing out his pitiful financial position and pressing his claims. It was a long winter; he was not invited to visit the court until May, 1505.

PART VI

Death

CHAPTER 18

"GLORIOUS MEMORY"

THE Admiral traveled by mule to Segovia, where he was granted an audience with King Ferdinand in early August. The king received him courteously, but would not agree to all of Columbus' claims. He suggested that the whole matter be settled by arbitration and readily approved as arbiter Diego de Deza, Archbishop of Seville, an old friend of the Admiral's. However, when Columbus learned that the king wished to arbitrate his titles as well as the claims for revenue, he stubbornly refused. The audience ended on this note, and he spent his last remaining months following the court as it moved first to Salamanca and then to Valladolid.

In May, 1506, Columbus' health failed rapidly. The weakening Admiral knew that his end was near, and called for the will he had written in his own hand at Segovia. With notaries and servants present as witnesses, he ratified the will on May 19. His friends and members of the family gathered at his bedside the next day. Christopher Columbus, ever a pious man, received the holy sacrament and breathed his last, saying, "Into thy hands, O Lord, I commit my spirit." Appropriately, that day, May 20, 1506, was Ascension Day.

The remains of Christopher Columbus traveled almost as much as the explorer did when he was alive. First his body was buried at Valladolid, but a few years later his son Diego moved the casket to Seville. He placed it in the monastery of Las Cuevas, where it remained for about thirty years. After that time the bodies of the Admiral and Don Diego (who had been buried beside his father) were transferred to Santo Domingo, Hispaniola, and re-entombed in the new cathedral there. In 1795, when Santo Domingo was given to France, the descendants of Columbus moved his remains to Cuba, so that he could continue to rest on Spanish soil. During the twentieth century this casket was shipped back to Spain for reinterment in Seville. There is some dispute that the proper remains made those last two journeys. In 1877, when the cathedral in Santo Domingo was repaired, another casket of the Columbus family was found. This one, it is now believed, contained the remains of the Admiral, while the one back at Seville contained the body of his son Diego. In either case, his memory is suitably honored.

It is typical of Columbus' life that he died and was buried almost unnoticed, and that his name was honored later. Most of his funds were in escrow when he died, but he stubbornly drew up a will that would have done credit to the wealthiest Spanish nobleman. He admitted that his estate was imaginary unless his claims were acknowledged by the crown. Actually he could have become one of the world's richest men if the Spanish rulers had honored their articles of agreement. Columbus never forgot that document, drawn up in April, 1492, in which their Highnesses granted him "the tenth part of the whole" of all merchandise, gold, pearls, and precious stones acquired from his Admiralty. Although he never enjoyed wealth, Columbus drew tremendous satisfaction from his titles of Admiral and Viceroy. He had the sovereigns' written agreement that he could "call and entitle" himself Don Christopher, as could "his sons and successors."

Columbus left everything to his legitimate son and principal heir, Diego, and the male issue of his house. Should this line expire, the estate was to pass, in turn, to Ferdinand, and, if defaulted, to Columbus' brother Bartholomew. If all these failed to produce male descendants, the estate would then pass to the female lines in like manner.

After his father died, Diego Columbus became the second admiral of the oceans. He brought suit against the crown for restitution of the family honors. Eventually, after he had been governor of Santo Domingo for several years, Diego got his wish. In 1520, King Charles reinstated him as "Viceroy over the Indies." In a later suit which was continued by Diego's widow in behalf of their son Luis Columbus, the family abandoned claims to island revenues in favor of a large estate in Veragua. The title "Viceroy of the Indies" was changed to "Duke of Veragua." This latter title has suffered many vicissitudes, including a thirty-year lawsuit, but it is valid today.

Christopher Columbus was a man of great contrasts. After a hard stretch at sea when his exhausted crew lay asleep, he would tiptoe around them, making adjustments to sails and rigging quietly, and let them sleep.

Yet in spite of his tenderness, he could execute a mutineer with impunity. At one time he might think of the Indians of the Caribbean as "noble savages," but a short while later he would send hundreds to the slave marts. He was one of the greatest practical seamen in the age of sail, and a capable leader of great fleets of ships. However, he turned out to be a weak administrator, whose settlement sites were poorly chosen and whose people mutinied against him.

Columbus was blindly loyal to the members of his family, and they, in turn, were fiercely devoted to him. Bartholomew, the adelantado, was a courageous leader and a good seaman and fighter, who supported the Admiral constantly. Not as effective but equally loyal, brother Diego, who longed for priesthood and not adventure, served Columbus well, and stubbornly stood up to Roldan's mutineers during dark days on Hispaniola. The great explorer spent the better part of his latter years in a series of efforts to protect his titles and estates for his descendants. In this, as in other ventures where stubborn determination eventually won out, he was successful.

Some of Columbus' biographers assert that his fertile mind bordered on the edge of insanity. They cite his religious fervor and the wanderings of his writing as examples. It is true that he was deeply religious; Ferdinand observed this on the fourth voyage, and it is very evident in his letters. However, as he grew older, the great explorer abandoned logical reason for inspiration and claimed to be a messenger of God with divine guidance. In this respect he may have been a bit fey, but this did not affect his ability to steer a straight course or to "smell" a hurricane when no one else could.

It is best to evaluate the man by what he accomplished,

and not by his peculiarities. Many great men of history have been lame, deaf, epileptic, or on the borderline of insanity. Despite his faults, in his own field of exploration Columbus towers over other men. He may not have realized the magnitude of his accomplishments, nor the tremendous impact that they would have on civilization, but he had the strength of his convictions and the personal courage to carry them out. Of all the accolades that his many biographers have given him, none is more appropriate than that of Samuel E. Morison, who said, ". . . no other sailor had the persistence, the knowledge and the sheer guts to sail thousands of miles into an unknown ocean until he found land. This was the most spectacular and most far-reaching geographical discovery in recorded human history."

The first voyage of discovery was the most important event of Columbus' life, and his greatest contribution to civilization. But his other voyages were significant too. A brief summary of each of these historic explorations, made in unknown waters with flimsy ships, serves as a testimonial to this great sailor's ability:

First Voyage —Discovered "America." Explored Bahamas, north coast of Cuba, and north coast of Haiti.

Second Voyage—Discovered windward and leeward islands that bound the eastern Caribbean, explored Puerto Rico, southern coast of Cuba, and Jamaica, and circumnavigated Hispaniola.

Third Voyage —Discovered Trinidad and South American continent, and explored coast of Venezuela.

Fourth Voyage—Discovered Central America and explored coasts of Honduras, Nicaragua, Costa Rica, and Panama.

A great part of his time in the New World was spent ashore administering colonial affairs. He had little training for this calling and was evidently out of his depth. But at sea he was supreme. His nautical instincts and knowledge, acquired over a lifetime of following the ,sea, carried him through four of the most difficult and daring voyages of exploration in the age of sail.

Often maligned and ridiculed, yet proud and dignified nonetheless, Columbus had a touch of greatness. This stubborn mariner brought the new and old worlds together. It is significant that one of his contemporaries, Diego Mendez, called him an "illustrious" man of "glorious memory." For almost five hundred years the world has honored this memory, and his name is a household word even today. One cannot help but think that somehow the astute old Admiral knew that it would turn out this way.

CHRONOLOGY
OF
CHRISTOPHER COLUMBUS (1451–1506)

EARLY LIFE

1451 (?)	Born in Genoa
1465	Goes to sea in Mediterranean
1476	Survives battle off Portugal and swims ashore at Lagos
1479	Marries Felipa Moniz de Perestrello in Lisbon
1480	Diego Columbus born in Porto Santo, Madeira
1482	Moves to Funchal, continues merchant sailing
1482 (?)	Corresponds with Toscanelli
1484	Proposes westward passage to King John of Portugal
1485	Felipa dies; King John disapproves voyage; Christopher takes son Diego to Spain
1486	Has audience with Queen Isabella and King Ferdinand
1488	Beatriz de Arana bears illegitimate son, Ferdinand Columbus
1492	In April, Spanish sovereigns agree to voyage, sign contracts. In August, sails from Palos, Spain, with *Niña*, *Pinta*, and *Santa Maria*

FIRST VOYAGE

Sept., 1492	Takes departure, begins ocean crossing; on 16th, enters Sargasso Sea
Oct.	Landfall at island of San Salvador on 12th
Oct.–Nov.	Cruises Bahama Islands and coast of Cuba
Dec.	Cruises northern coast of Haiti

Dec.	On 25th, *Santa Maria* grounds on reef east of Cap Haitien; Columbus establishes settlement, names it "Navidad"
Jan., 1493	*Niña* and *Pinta* sail along northern coast of Hispaniola; on 16th, return voyage begins
Feb.	*Niña* and *Pinta* separated by storms
Mar.	*Niña* arrives at Lisbon on 4th; on 15th, *Niña* returns to Palos and *Pinta* arrives

SECOND VOYAGE

Sept., 1493	Sails from Cádiz with seventeen ships on 24th
Nov.	Landfall at Dominica Island on 3rd; discovers Leeward Islands on 4th; sails through them to site of Navidad, Hispaniola
Dec.	Moves east along Haitian coast
Jan., 1494	Enters harbor and founds new settlement, Isabella, on 2nd
Apr.	Commences new voyage of discovery to the west on 24th; on 29th, lands at Cape Maisi and claims Cuba for Spain
May	Anchors in St. Ann's Bay, Jamaica, on 5th; on 13th, sails north to Cuba and commences exploration of southern coast
	Enters "Bahia de Cochinos" (Bay of Pigs) on 26th
June	On 12th, makes crew take oath that Cuba is part of Asian mainland
	Turns back
July	Anchors in Montego Bay, Jamaica, on 21st; explores coasts of Jamaica
Aug.–Sept.	Explores coast of Hispaniola. Returns to Isabella gravely ill on Sept. 29
Mar., 1496	Starts home with *Niña* and *India*
June	Arrives in Cádiz on 11th

THIRD VOYAGE

June, 1497	Sovereigns approve third voyage
May, 1498	Departs San Lucar on 30th, with six ships, for Canary Islands via Madeira
June	Divides fleet, takes three to Cape Verde Islands, sends three direct to Hispaniola
July	Begins third crossing on 4th; makes landfall at Trinidad on 31st
Aug.	Explores Gulf of Paria; discovers South America on 13th; arrives at Alta Vela, off Hispaniola on 20th; anchors at Santo Domingo on 31st
Oct., 1500	Bobadilla arrests Columbus and sends him back to Spain in chains

FOURTH VOYAGE

May, 1502	Sails from Cádiz with four ships on 11th, arrives Canary Islands on 20th
June	On 29th, arrives Santo Domingo
July	Departs Hispaniola for Central America on 14th; on 30th, reaches coast of Honduras
Oct.	Arrives at Veragua, finds gold
Nov.	Explores coast of Panama
Jan., 1503	Returns to Veragua, searches for gold
Apr.	Departs Veragua, heads south
May	Leaves Panamanian coast, heads for Cuba
June, 1503– June, 1504	Marooned in Jamaica
June, 1504	Sails for Santo Domingo on 28th
Sept.	Departs for Spain
Nov.	Arrives at San Lucar

LAST YEARS

Nov., 1504	On 26th, Queen Isabella dies
May, 1505	Columbus visits King Ferdinand, demands restoration of revenues
May, 1506	Columbus dies on 20th

BIBLIOGRAPHY

Columbus, Ferdinand. *The Life of the Admiral Christopher Columbus by His Son Ferdinand*, tr. by Benjamin Keen. New Brunswick, New Jersey: Rutgers University Press, 1959.

Donworth, Albert B. *Why Columbus Sailed*, 2nd ed. rev. New York: Exposition Press, 1953.

Fiske, John. *The Discovery of America*. 2 vols. Boston: Riverside Press, 1892.

Herrmann, Paul. *The Great Age of Discovery*, tr. by Arnold J. Pomerans. New York: Harper & Row, Inc., 1958.

Irving, Washington. *The Life and Voyages of Christopher Columbus*. 3 vols., rev. ed. New York: G. P. Putnam's Sons, 1861.

Jane, Cecil. *Select Documents Illustrating the Four Voyages of Columbus*. Printed for the Hakluyt Society. London: University Press, 1930–33.

Kayserling, M. *Christopher Columbus*, tr. by Charles Gross. New York: Longmans, Green and Company, 1894.

Las Casas, Bartolomé de. *Historia General de las Indias*. Madrid: M. Ginesta, 1875. (From a manuscript written during 1527–61.)

Major, R. H., ed. *Christopher Columbus' Four Voyages to the*

New World, Letters and Selected Documents, rev. ed. New York: Corinth Books, 1961.

Morison, Samuel E. *Admiral of the Ocean Sea*. Boston: Little, Brown and Company, 1942.

——. *Christopher Columbus, Mariner*. Boston and Toronto: Little, Brown and Company, 1955.

——. *Journals and Other Documents on the Life and Voyages of Christopher Columbus*. New York: The Heritage Press, 1963.

Nunn, George E. *The Geographical Conceptions of Columbus*. New York: American Geographical Society, 1924.

Tarducci, Francisco. *The Life of Christopher Columbus*, tr. by Henry F. Brownson. 2 vols. Detroit: Henry F. Brownson, 1890. (Note: Brownson was both translator and publisher.)

Thacher, John B. *Christopher Columbus, His Life, His Work, His Remains*. 3 vols. New York: G. P. Putnam's Sons, 1903–4.

Winsor, Justin. *Christopher Columbus—and How He Received and Imparted the Spirit of Discovery*. Cambridge: Cambridge University Press, 1891.

INDEX

Africa, 9, 11, 14
Aguado, Juan, 100
Aguja (Spanish ship), 136, 137
Alexander VI, Pope, 75
Alfonso V, King of Portugal, 14
Alliarcus, Petrus, 13
Alphonso V of Aragon, 6
Alta Vela, 117
Amazon River, discovery of, 130
Aragon, 19, 20
Arana, Beatriz Enríquez de, 22–23
Aristotle, 12
Azores, ix, 66, 67
Azua, 136–137

Babeque (Great Inagua), 57–58, 86
Bacon, Roger, 12–13
Bahamas, 50, 52–53
Bahia Bariay, 54
Bahia de Cochinos (Bay of Pigs), 90
Bahia de las Flechas (Bay of Arrows), 63
Bahia de las Vacas (Portland Bight), 93
Balboa, Vasco Nuñez de, 140
Ballester, Miguel, 119, 121, 122
Barahona, 119
Barcelona, 71

Barcelona Maritime Museum, 30
Barrantes, Garcia de, 122
Bay Islands, 138
Behechio, 98
Bermuda (Spanish ship), 133, 135, 136, 148
Bernaldez, Andres, 105
Biblioteca Colombina, 13
Boa Vista, 110
Bobadilla, Francisco de, 124–125, 130, 135–137
"Book of Privileges," Columbus, 131
Boquerón Bay, 80
Brazil, discovery of, 129–130
Buil, Fray, 95

Cabot, Sebastian, 45
Canary Islands, 9, 34, 41, 78
Caonabo, 97–99
Cape Cruz, 87, 91, 92
Cape Engano, 93
Cape Gracias a Dios (Thanks to God), 139, 140
Cape Maisi, 86
Cape Nombre de Dios, 143
Cape Samana, 63
Cape Tiburon (Cape San Miguel), 93, 152
Cape Verde Islands, 75
Carib Indians, 58, 79–80, 96, 101

Caribbean Islands, 43, 63
Caribbean Sea, 131
Carvajal, Captain, 121
Castile, 19, 20
Catholic faith, 76
Celestial navigation, 33
Central America, 131, 149
Chanca, Dr., 77, 78, 80, 81, 82
Charles, King of Spain, 163
Charles VIII, King of France, 23
China, 13, 14
Christianity, 25, 35
Cipangu. *See* Japan
Columbus, Bartholomew
    (brother), 4, 109, 132, 138,
    139, 144, 152–154, 156, 157,
    163
    as adelantado of Hispaniola,
      118–120, 141
    early life in Lisbon, 7–8
    imprisonment of, 125
    as leader of Veragua settle-
      ment, 145–146
    relationship with Christopher,
      23, 94, 96–97, 117, 164
Columbus, Christopher:
    as administrator, 27, 83, 95–96,
      164, 166
    birthplace of, 3–5
    burial of, 162
    death of, xi, 161–162
    early childhood of, 5
    education of, 7, 10, 11
    financial affairs of, 130, 157,
      162
    imprisonment of, 124–125
    last will of, 4, 11, 23, 108, 161,
      162
    literary works about, ix–x
    as mapmaker, 6, 34
    navigation of, 33–34, 41, 109
    personality and temperament

of, x, 7, 10, 22, 27, 91, 96,
    163–164
physical appearance of, 10
poor health of, 67, 82, 88, 93–
    94, 115, 132, 139, 149, 164
quoted: at time of death, 162;
    on Iceland voyage, 16; on
    natives, 51, 60, 112; pre-
    amble to journal of first
    voyage, 40–41; on speaking
    with God, 146–147
religion of, 35, 53, 105, 131,
    132, 133, 146, 164
as seaman, xi, 6, 27, 39, 52, 88,
    109, 132, 139, 164, 166
as writer, ix, 131, 133, 157, 164
Columbus, Diego (brother), 3,
    76–77, 83, 84, 93, 95, 96, 98,
    120, 124, 164
Columbus, Diego (son), 4, 11,
    19, 21, 23, 34, 67, 77, 108,
    157, 162, 163
Columbus, Domenico (father),
    3–4
Columbus, Felipa Moniz de Per-
    estrello (wife), 10–11, 109,
    134
    death of, 17
Columbus, Ferdinand (son), 5,
    7, 11, 12, 16, 67, 77, 93, 108,
    115, 133, 163
    as biographer, 23, 88, 152
    birth of, 22
    during fourth voyage, 132,
      139
    quoted: on Columbus' prep-
      arations for fourth voyage,
      133; on Columbus' treat-
      ment of Indians, 51; on
      thunderstorms during sec-
      ond voyage, 89–90
Columbus, Luis (grandson), 163

Columbus, Susanna (mother), 3
Cook, Captain James, 33
Cordova, 21–22
Cosa, Juan de la, 30, 61, 77, 123
Costa Rica, 140, 141
Cuba, 84, 138, 148, 162
    Columbus' first tour of, 50–58
    Columbus' second tour of, 85–91
    first Spanish settlement in, 58

Deza, Diego de (Archbishop of Seville), 161
Dias, Bartholomew, 23
Diaz, Bernal, 83
Dominica, 78–79
Dragon's Mouth (Boca del Dragon), 114–115

Eratosthenes, 13
Ericson, Leif, x
Escobar, Diego de, 155–156
Escobedo, Rodrigo de, 51
"Exploration by certification," 91

Ferdinand Columbus. See Columbus, Ferdinand
Ferdinand, King of Spain, 19–20, 24, 29, 48, 70–71, 75, 98, 130, 157, 161
Fernandina (Long Island), 53
Fieschi, Bartolomeo, 152–153
Fonseca, Don Juan de, 76, 108, 123, 125
Fort Conceptión, 119–120
Four Great Voyages of Columbus, The, map, 47

Gama, Vasco da, 129

Genoa, 3, 4
    mariners of, 6
Granada, 19, 24, 115
Great Khan, 35, 54, 85, 132
Guacanagari, 61–62, 63, 81, 85, 98
Guacanayabo, 89
Guantanamo, 86
Guatiguana, 97, 98
Guevara, Fernando de, 123–124
Gulf of Paria (Golfo de la Ballena), 111–112, 113, 123
Gulf of Pearls, 114, 116, 123
Gutierrez, Pedro, 49
Guzman, Don Enrique de, 21

Haiti, 52, 58, 72, 148, 152
Harana, Diego de, 63, 81
Harrisse, Henry, ix
Henry VII, King of England, 23
Henry the Navigator, Prince, 9, 10
Hispaniola, 59–63, 80, 88, 93, 106, 117, 130, 131, 134, 135, 148
    Indian rebellion in, 95–101
    Spanish rebellion in, 119–122
Hojeda, Alonso de, 84, 99, 115, 123, 130, 147
Honduras, 138–139
Humboldt, Baron von, x

Iceland, 16
Imago Mundi, Alliarcus, 13
Indians, 58–59, 63–64, 86, 87, 89, 92, 114, 138, 141–143
    Columbus' treatment of, 56, 96–97
    encounter with on fourth voyage, 145–146
    of Jamaica, 150, 152, 155

naming of, 51
rebellion of Tainos Indians, 95–100
of Trinidad, 112–113
Isabella, city of, 83–84, 93, 94, 97, 99, 100, 109, 118, 120
founding of, 82
Isabella (Crooked Island), 53, 54, 57
Isabella, Queen of Spain, ix, 20–22, 23, 28, 51, 53, 70, 71, 97, 106, 108, 125, 130, 132
death of, 157
physical appearance of, 20
support of first voyage, 19–20, 24–25
Islas de Arena (Ragged Island), 53
Isle of Pines, 91

Jamaica, 87, 92, 93, 138
Columbus' stay in, 148–156
Japan, 13, 15, 34, 48, 54, 72, 84
Jardin de la Reina. See Queen's Garden
John, King of Portugal, 17–18, 43, 69, 72, 75
Juan, Prince, 34, 106, 108

La Bella Saonese, 93
La Capitana (Spanish ship), 133, 136, 138, 141, 144, 146, 148
La Gallega (Spanish ship), 133, 136, 144, 147
La Huerta (The Garden), 141
La Navidad, 62–63, 82, 85, 145
Indian attack on, 81
La Ribida, 21, 23, 24
Las Casas, Bartolome de, 11, 16, 56
Las Cuevas, 162
Las Palacios, 105

Las Palmas, 42, 134
Ledesma, Pedro de, 156
"Letter of the First Voyage," 70–71
Lettera Rarissima, 151
Lisbon, 7, 8, 9–10, 32

Magellan, Ferdinand, 14
Marchena, Brother Antonio de, 21
Margarit, Pedro, 95
Margarita (Island), 115
Margarita, Princess of Austria, 106
Marie Galante, 79, 100
"Mariegalante," 77
Martins, Fernam, 14–15
Medina Celi, Luis de la Cerda, Duke of, 21
Mediterranean Sea, 6
Mendez, Diego, 145, 149–150, 151–153, 155, 156
Mohammedans, 19
Mona Passage, 93
Monte Cristi, 81
Montego Bay, 87, 92
Moors, 19, 22, 133–134
Morison, Samuel Eliot, 5, 33, 165
Morocco, 133
Moxica, Adrian de, 123–124
Murdoch, Lieutenant J. B., 50
Mutiny, in Jamaica during fourth voyage, 153–154, 156

Nacaona, 153
Navidad. See La Navidad
New Isabella. See Santo Domingo
New World, x, 14, 19, 51, 75, 116, 166
Nicaragua, 140, 141

Niña, 14, 29–30, 31–32, 39, 46, 61, 63, 66, 67, 68–69, 77, 90, 92, 100
Niño, Pedro Alonzo, 34, 130, 147
Nippon, 13
North America, 117, 131

Orient, westward passage to, xi, 8, 12, 131
Orinoco River, 111
Ovando, Nicholas de, 130, 135–137, 153, 155, 157
Oviedo, 5

Pacific Ocean, discovery of, 140
Palos, 25, 28–30, 39, 41, 70
Panama, 140, 148
Panama Canal, 143
"Pearl Coast," 115
Penalosa, Juan de, 29
Perestrello, Bartholomew, 10–11
Perez, Alonzo, 111
Perez, Friar Juan, 23–24, 28, 35
Pinta, 14, 30, 31–32, 34, 41–42, 49, 57, 63, 66, 70
Pinzón, Francisco Martín, 34
Pinzón, Martín Alonzo, 23, 29, 32, 34, 41–42, 46, 49, 57, 63, 70
Pinzón, Vicente Yanez, 29, 32, 34, 42, 129–130
Polo, Marco, 13, 14, 54
Ponce de León, Juan, 77
Porras, Francisco de, 132, 153–154, 156
Port St. Nicholas, 58
Portland Bight. *See* Bahia de las Vacas
Porto Bello, 143, 147
Porto Blanca, 63
Porto Conceptión, 59

Porto Paz (Port de Paix), 59
Porto Principe, 57
Porto St. Thomas (Acul Bay), 60
Porto Santo, 10, 11, 12, 58, 109
Portugal, 9, 32, 43, 75, 129, 132, 134
  Columbus' stay in, 9–18
Ptolemy, 12, 13
Puerto Brazil (Jacmel), 138
Puerto Bueno, 87
Puerto Rico, 80
Punta de la Plaza (Erin Point), 112
Punta Escuda Blanca, 115

Queen's Garden, 88–89, 92, 138, 148
Quibian, 144–145

René, King of Anjou, 6–7
Rio Belen, 144
Rolan, Bartolomeo, 34
Roldan, 119–124, 136, 137, 164
Ruiz, Sancho, 34

St. Ann's Bay, 148–156
St. John, 80
St. Thomas, 80
San Miguel, 67
San Salvador, 50–52, 98
Sanchez, Rodrigo, 49
Sandy Point (Punta del Arenal), 112
Santa Clara, 67
Santa Clara de Moguer, 66
Santa Maria, 7, 14, 30–32, 33, 42, 48
  replica of, in Washington, D.C., 30
  shipwreck of, 61–62

Santa Maria de Guadalupe, 66

Santa Maria de Guadeloupe (island), 79

Santa Maria de la Concepción (Rum Cay), 53

Santa Maria de Loretto, 66

Santangel, Luis de, 24–25

Santo Domingo, 109–110, 117, 118–125, 134, 135, 150, 152, 157, 162

Sargasso Sea, 45, 78

Savona, 3, 4, 93

Serpent's Mouth (Boca de la Sierpe), 113

Ships, fifteenth-century, 31

Slavery, 82–83, 97–98, 99, 122, 132, 164

South America, 111–112, 117, 131

Spain, Inquisition in, 20

Spanish court, ix, 24–25, 70, 105–106, 161

Tainos Indians, 95

Talavera, Fernando de, 22, 24

Tanamo Bay, 56, 57, 58

Teran, Jose Maria Martinez-Hidalgo y, 30

Terreros, Pedro de, 135

Tobacco, discovery of, 55–56

Tobago, 115

Torres, Antonio de, 83, 98

Torres, Luis de, 35, 54–55, 56

Tortuga, 59

Toscanelli, Paolo, 14–16, 34

Triana, Rodrigo de, 49

Trinidad, 111

Tristan, Diego, 146

Venezuela, 123, 147

Veragua, 142–143, 144, 147, 148, 163

Veragua, Spanish Duke of, ix

Vespucci, Amerigo, 116, 123

Vieques, 80

Villa, Pedro de, 66

Vizcaina (Spanish ship), 133, 136, 137, 148

Voyages of Columbus:
First:
crew, 32, 34–35; attitude of, 43, 45–46, 65
discovery and naming of places, 53, 56
effect on medieval Europe, 51–52
financing, 25
first landing, 50–51
first sight of land, 48–49, 71
provisions, 35
purposes, 35, 40–41, 55
return, 65–70
route, 43–44, 52
ships, 29–32. See also Niña, Pinta, Santa Maria
summary of, 165
Second:
crew, 76–77
departure, 78
discovery and naming of places, 80, 93
illness during, 82
return, 100–101
route, 78
royal instructions, 75–76
summary of, 165
Third:
difficulties in doldrums, 110
discovery and naming of places, 111–112, 113, 114
fleet, 109
preparation, 108
route, 109–111

Voyages of Columbus: Second (*Continued*)
  summary of, 165
Fourth:
  crew, 133
  departure, 133–134
  disastrous storm, 136–137
  discovery and naming of places, 141
  Indian rebellion, 145–146
  return, 157
  route, 133–134
  royal instructions, 131
  settlement in Veragua, 144–145
  ships, 133
  summary of, 166
Iceland (1477), 16–17

Watling's Island, 50
Windward Passage, 58, 92, 93

Xaragua, 119, 120–121, 122, 153
Xerez, Rodrigo de, 54–55, 56